THE COMPLETE
MARTIAL ARTS

THE COMPLETE
MARTIAL ARTS

PAUL CROMPTON

McGRAW-HILL PUBLISHING COMPANY

New York St. Louis San Francisco Bogota Hamburg Madrid Mexico
Milan Paris Sao Paulo Tokyo

This book was created and produced by
Roxby Productions Limited
A division of Roxby Press Limited
126 Victoria Rise
London SW4 0NW
United Kingdom

Editor: Gilly Abrahams
Design: Geoff Power, Powers Design
Photography: Charles Best
Sumo Photography: Takashi Imoto
Indian Martial Arts Photography: Luis Tarmillo
Typesetting: Hobbs the Printers of Southampton, England
Origination: J Film Process

Library of Congress Cataloging-in-Publication Data
Crompton, Paul H., 1936 –
    The complete martial arts / by Paul Crompton.
        p.   cm.
    ISBN 0-07-014450-8   : $24.95
    1. Martial arts   I. Title
GV1101.C75   1989
796.8– –dc20
                                                                        89–8121
                                                                        CIP

ISBN 0-07-014450-8

1   2   3   4   5   6   7   8   9   xxx   xxx   8   9   2   1   0   9
Printed and bound in Yugoslavia

CONTENTS

KARATE

Karate, meaning 'empty hand', originated in Okinawa, an island to the south-west of Japan. Originally it was meant to be used to kill one's enemy with a single blow, hence the emphasis on maximum power, perfect technique and focus of blow. Today, most of the training halls or dojo in

Opposite page: karate students engaged in freestyle training.
Below: a typical high block against a punch to the face.
Above right: a variation on a high block, using the open hand.
Right: a low arm block against a front kick.
Below right: the man on the right is delivering a ridge-hand blow, using the inside edge of his hand against the head of his opponent.

the West are following a Japanese style or ryu, although Okinawan forms are still well known and respected.

Karate was introduced to the Japanese mainland by an educationalist, Gichin Funakoshi, from Okinawa. He was invited to give a demonstration in Tokyo in 1922, and within two years karate was part of the university curriculum. Like judo, karate has undergone a dramatic change in approach. In its Okinawan form there were no competitions, and in its early days in Japan there was still an absence of the sporting element. Students trained in pre-arranged sequences of movement or kata, and in techniques; they also underwent training to improve their stamina and strength. Funakoshi's best pupils eventually started their own dojo, modified some of the techniques, and developed their own styles. In the 1970s karate became hugely popular in the West, swept in on the tide of success surrounding kung fu star Bruce Lee. Schools were set up all over the world, offering several dozen styles of karate, but basically it is still an empty-hand art using kicks, blocks and punches. Although there are some throwing techniques, principally a leg sweep used in sport karate to bring an opponent to the floor or knock him off balance, on the whole it remains an art of striking, not grappling.

Modern karate can be divided into three basic categories: traditional karate, sport karate and full-contact karate. Sport karate slowly emerged over the last 25 years; the more advanced students needed something to strive for, other than technical excellence and understanding, and dojo all over the world began to stage competitions. The fundamental rule in such competitions was that there could be no contact. Western students, in the main, would not put up with being punched and kicked like the bare-knuckle bruisers of the nineteenth century. To

Opposite page, left: *the man on the left uses a powerful rising elbow blow against his opponent's chin or side of the jaw.*

Opposite page, right: *a variation on what is popularly known as the 'karate chop'. In this knife-hand technique, the narrow edge of the hand 'cuts' into the opponent's neck.*

Below left: *in the hammer-fist technique, the clenched fist is used like a hammer or club, in this case against the back of an opponent. The left hand grips his jacket, pulling him forward and down, making him vulnerable to this technique.*

Below right: *the man on the left demonstrates a straight, lunging punch to the face, like a sword thrust. In some ways it resembles the classic straight left (or right) of boxing.*

score a point a participant had to deliver a punch or kick with sufficient exactness and sufficiently near the target for it to be judged effective if it had landed. Wilful hitting of an opponent brought disqualification. This restriction, while safeguarding the lives and limbs of the students, led to the use of techniques which, in the opinion of die-hard traditionalists, would not have crushed an indolent fly. Traditional stances and rock-like hardness were sacrificed for speed of attack. Students who clung to the past said that if hit by such a punch or kick a tough karate man would almost ignore it and would finish off the 'attacker' with a powerful, well-supported traditional reply. Two camps were thus formed, admittedly with some overlap, and they prepared the way for a third.

A few years after the advent of competition karate, kick boxing began to make its appearance (see page 180) and taking a leaf from the same book, several really tough karate schools began to stage full-contact karate tournaments, some using protective fist and leg guards, others using no protection at all. At the same time the Korean karate schools (see taekwondo, page 166) were experimenting with full-contact events for which specially designed body armour, gloves, shin guards and padded boots were worn. A number of variations on the theme of fighting and really hitting emerged therefore, each school creating its own international governing body and its own rules.

Meanwhile, the traditional karate students trudged on. Some of them occasionally took part in tournaments, within or outside their own organizations, but for the most part the emphasis remained on kata, techniques, and research into older forms; they clung to the past, trying to follow the samurai ideal of obedience, respect for the chief instructor, and integrity of style.

Before joining a karate club it is advisable to enquire along what lines it is run. It may not fit into any of the three categories with clear-cut exactness, but at least you should be able to find out where the emphasis lies.

What then is karate? It is a method of fighting without the aid of a weapon. Head, shoulders, elbows, fists, wrists, knuckles, fingers, edge of the hand, knee, heel, toe and instep may all be used. That is to say, within the syllabus of a given karate style techniques using all parts of the body may be found. In full-contact and sport karate the highest scoring technique is the reverse punch – the equivalent, in boxing terms, of a right-handed punch delivered by a man standing in the orthodox stance: left hand leading, right hand back. This fact underlines the traditional karate student's contention that

Opposite page: one of the most powerful karate kicks, the roundhouse. The man performing the kick brings his right leg from behind his body in a circular action, then uses either the ball or the top of his foot to strike. This is not an easy kick to stop.

Top: a side, thrusting kick, using the edge or sole of the foot. Great care must be taken when using this technique or the attacker will lose his balance as he makes contact.

Above: the man on the left performs a simple front thrusting kick to the abdomen or solar plexus. In sport karate this form of kicking technique is one of the most commonly used; it scores high points.

11

Above: the study of karate involves the study of kata, pre-arranged sequences of movement which demonstrate and combine the techniques of the style concerned. Here a student shows two distinctive movements from such kata.

Opposite page, above left: two students engage in freestyle sparring. The man on the right has just successfully blocked a kick from his partner.

Opposite page, above right: during freestyle sparring, the man on the left tries a front kick which his partner blocks with his forearm.

Opposite page, below left: the man on the right takes up a position often seen during freestyle sparring. He arches his body up and away from an attack, at the same time raising his arms to defend himself. As in all martial arts sparring, the students try to see, a split second in advance, what the opponent will do. They are not always able to do this accurately, and may leave themselves wide open to the real attack.

Opposite page, below right: the man on the right tries a roundhouse kick to the body, which his partner successfully smothers.

Top left: *throwing with the hands is not common in karate contests, but it does happen. Here the man on the right has been hoisted up and is about to be 'dumped' on his back.*
Centre left: *students do calisthenics and stretching exercises alone or in pairs. Here one student helps another with a 'bridge' exercise for the back.*
Below left: *a leg-stretching exercise performed solo.*
Centre right: *the man on the left is stretching his leg by resting it on his partner's shoulder.*
Below right: *push-ups with clenched fists to strengthen the arms and body and toughen up the knuckles.*

sport karate leads to a dilution of the art of karate and to a potential loss of knowledge of other techniques, since the sport karate student's main aim is to win. In order to win he will cultivate winning techniques, at the expense of the rest.

Kicks and punches are divided into three levels: those which aim at the head, between head and waist, and below the waist. In sport karate, a high standard of fitness is needed, plus a flexible and elastic body. In the traditional and full-contact sides of the art, there is much greater emphasis on strength, since a student is expected to stand punishment, should the need arise. Some schools also emphasize toughening up the body by striking hard surfaces, driving the hands into containers of sand or pebbles; one group of karate students in England train not at pumping iron but punching iron! Another training method, not very widespread but certainly found in the West, is to allow wooden sticks, sometimes quite thick, to be broken across the body or the arms. This is seen as a test of toughness and correct stance training. To improve strength and technique karate students often train in the sea or in lakes, waist deep in water, or on rough, sloping ground to improve their balance.

Karate has fired the imagination of many men and women, and accordingly they have sought conditions and types of training which fit their image of the art. Breaking techniques belong in this category. The idea of breaking hard substances using only the bare hands or feet is far older than karate, but the variety of objects that are broken surely belongs to the late twentieth century, inspired by the fledgling karate men of the 1960s. Blocks of wood, roof tiles, huge blocks of ice, large pebbles and composite building blocks are all used, and any of these items may be doused in petrol and smashed while blazing furiously. Sometimes, even more extraordinarily, building bricks have been broken by a head butt. When the sensationalism attending such feats had died down, karate men slowly withdrew from breaking techniques as a feature of their training and public demonstrations, and this particular skill is now mainly displayed by taekwondo students.

One of the best-known karate masters is Masatatsu Oyama. This incredibly tough man actually fought several bulls with his bare hands and, using a karate technique, broke off their horns. His training was rigorously hard, and by all accounts he drove himself and his students to an extent unsurpassed by any other teacher. Many karate masters stress perfection of technique rather than toughness, while others stress knowledge of kata, so that within the framework of karate a student can find enormous variety.

The study of kata can be absorbing. Some of these sequences of movement were native to Okinawa; others evolved from Chinese kung fu, brought back to Okinawa by travellers or by karate teachers who had gone abroad in search of new techniques. Kata may be based on the movements of birds or animals or simply teach the combination of some of the most basic karate movements. Others are performed very slowly, a little like dynamic tension exercises, with concentration on co-ordinated breathing and the development of force. Each master within a particular style may have introduced slight changes in the way a kata is done, but on the whole the structures of traditional kata remain inviolate. People who study kata deeply and are filled with respect for them believe that they should not be changed as they are part of the karate heritage. Just as one would not dream of changing a famous painting or piece of sculpture, one should not change a kata; invent a new one if you like but preserve the original as it was. Each kata movement, performed solo, has an application to combat and part of the study is to discover how a particular movement of a new kata is applied. Is it a block, a throw, a punch, a kick, a lock or an evasion?

Part of the discipline of kata performance is to finish on the exact spot where you began. Kata competitions are held as part of every karate tournament. Four judges sit at the corners of a large square. The competitor comes to the middle of the square and announces in a loud voice the name of the kata he is to perform. When he has finished, the judges hold up their score cards, marking him for correct technique, power of movement, correct focus of a strike, timing, form, speed, and a host of different aspects which in the end come down to a decision based on experience.

As in most of the martial arts, it must be emphasized that karate is not a system of self-defence as such. An expert in sport karate is not necessarily a tough man. His training has been aimed not at hitting people, but at scoring points, and unless he has been unfortunate he has not been hit much himself. There are men and women who can defend themselves using karate, but they have studied the techniques of karate as applied to self-defence situations.

Karate training is physically demanding. A class usually begins and ends with an exercise session and may last for up to two hours, so it is advisable to attain a certain degree of fitness before taking up the art. Most people who have done aerobics classes will probably be able to cope well with the rigours of training.

JUDO

Today, judo is essentially a competitive sport. Especially in the West, it has all the trappings of crowd participation and commercialization, and a win-at-all-costs outlook which its founder, Dr Jigoro Kano (1860–1938), wished to avoid. Kano, like several other famous martial arts masters, was very involved in education, and from an early age saw in his conception of judo a way of inculcating moral principles and physical wellbeing into the Japanese nation and later the world at large. He founded his judo centre in Tokyo in 1882 and called it the Kodokan. This place became almost a shrine for judo-ka (judo students) and its principles and methods underlay those of every offshoot, world-wide, until some 15 years after World War II. Japanese methods, etiquette and ideas, taken abroad by Japanese instructors, stamped every dojo with the Kodokan image. Then, gradually, as skilled judo-ka emerged in each foreign country, what were seen as the shackles and limitations of the native Japanese approach were shaken off. The once respected and even revered Japanese teachers were no longer invited to take up residence at the expense of the host club or judo association, and an essentially Western approach developed.

This new approach had good and bad elements. Among the bad elements was the growing imperative to win. Judo had always been put forward as a means of studying through training; a means of unifying mind and body. While this intention had never been followed universally, it was widely known. In the 1950s it was still customary for two judo opponents to stand up more or less straight while fighting, keeping the judo jacket tied down under the belt. To fight in a crouched position, as is now commonplace in the West, with the jacket flapping about and the belt hanging low down almost between the legs, was frowned on. Standing upright meant that you were more likely to be thrown, but so was your opponent; crouching meant that you were less likely to be thrown, but your technique suffered and your whole attitude became defensive. Many people lamented this type of change. On the plus side, Western methods of training, Western knowledge of muscle use and development, and a host of other contributions from the increasingly intensive study of sport in general helped the study of judo in particular.

Kano was originally a student of jujutsu. There were many styles of jujutsu in Japan in the nineteenth century. The traditional story told of Kano is that he sifted through the existing jujutsu

Opposite page: one of the most spectacular judo techniques, the stomach throw.
Top: students demonstrate a kneeling bow, part of the etiquette of judo.
Above: a standing bow before a contest. Note that both men keep their eyes on the opponent to avoid the possibility of a surprise attack.

styles, extracted the techniques which fitted his new concept and welded them into a system. As the system had to function as an art or 'do' form, all the fatal methods of the jujutsu styles had to be modified or discarded. He devised a comprehensive system of throwing, floor fighting, joint locking, striking and resuscitation. To safeguard the students, several methods of breaking the fall, and also making sure that your opponent landed safely, were included in the syllabus. In addition to the combative side of the art, a system of kata or pre-arranged movements which incorporated all the techniques of judo was evolved. The kata were carried out with one person performing the throws, for example, and the other person willingly allowing him to do them. In this way the correct method of carrying out a technique could be studied, without the additional problem of dealing with an opponent who is trying

The standard judo hold on the sleeve and 'lapel' of a partner's jacket. From this holding position, many of judo's standing throws can be readily performed.

According to the rules of judo, when the jacket becomes loose and is no longer held by the belt the contest should be stopped so that clothing can be adjusted.

to prevent you from doing so.

The underlying principle which was supposed to accompany all this activity can be described in a short story. One day a Japanese student was standing watching the snow fall. From time to time the snow accumulated on the branch of a tree to such an extent that the branch snapped off. But one tree in particular, the willow, always yielded before the crucial moment came, so its branches were preserved. This principle of yielding to force, and using an opponent's force, has always been quoted in connection with judo. It is a most difficult principle to follow, since one's usual inclination is to resist force with force. The exploration of this principle was part of Kano's desired judo discipline – a far cry from winning at all costs.

Today, the original elements of Kano's judo that are most widely studied are the throwing tech-

niques, breakfalling, joint locking and fighting on the ground. Beginners learn to break their fall and to take care of their partner; they also learn simple throws and hold-downs. One of the first benefits of judo training is better balance. Over the years, judo-ka become very skilful at staying on their feet, balancing on one leg and falling without fear. To a newcomer it often seems miraculous that bones are not broken every time a student hits the mat, flat on his back. But up he gets, none the worse for wear, and carries on fighting. Judo mats were originally made of rice straw, but nowadays they are usually made of dense foam, covered in cotton or plastic, which cushions the fall.

Judo is scientific in the sense that it uses simple laws of mechanics to produce its spectacular throws. A throw can be centred on any joint in the body. Mechanically, the body is in a sense weakest at its

A student demonstrates a judo breakfall, designed to enable him to take a fall without injury.

On page 16 this fall is being used in response to the stomach throw.

joints, so throws involving the shoulder, hip, knee and ankle are used. On the ground, the body can be pinned most effectively at the shoulders and hips, or at a 'corner', such as one shoulder or hip, so the judo range of hold-downs or 'pins' concentrates on methods of immobilizing these points. Locking the joints in a standing position is not generally done, since this is dangerous, but locking the joints on the floor is permitted. Strangling or choking is also permitted on the floor. This is not as dangerous as it sounds since you are expected to tap your opponent as a sign of submission to such an attack if you feel that it is more than you can bear.

Scoring in judo is straightforward. A clean throw wins a point; a passable throw wins half a point. An effective pin, lock, choke or strangle wins a point. However, scoring may vary from tournament to tournament.

The clothing worn in judo is called judo-gi and is usually made of unbleached cotton. Bleached cotton outfits are also available but are more expensive. The trousers are very baggy to permit freedom of movement on the floor. The jacket, which is heavily quilted to reduce impact and protect the skin from being rubbed on the mat, has no buttons, zips or toggles; it simply folds across the front of the body and is held in place by a heavy-duty belt which circles the body twice and is knotted at the front.

The well-known expression 'black belt' comes from judo. For some reason, possibly attributable to the popular press and fiction, a person qualified to wear a black belt is seen as someone who can, with a flick of his wrist, send the toughest thug flying over the rooftops. Certainly, in the West, the attainment of black belt status has always been a coveted achievement, but in Japan it was regarded

Opposite page, top left: a student tries a half-kneeling, X-strangulation technique, holding his partner's 'lapels' on both sides of the neck and drawing his arms outwards to compress the nerves and blood vessels.

Opposite page, top right: a rear choke-hold, using the jacket and the arm to cut off the passage of air to the windpipe. The attacker maintains a steady pressure until his partner submits or breaks free, or — in a contest — until the referee orders him to stop.

Opposite page, centre left: a popular arm lock against the elbow joint. The man on the floor has just been thrown on his back. His partner follows him down, pulls his left arm straight, then presses it down against his own inner thigh and applies pressure. At the same time his right leg prevents his partner from rising.

Opposite page, centre right: the man on his back is being held down by a T-hold. His partner presses down with his chest and holds on to the other man's jacket with both hands.

Opposite page, below: this is the classic judo scarf hold. The attacker presses his ribs against his partner, pins his head with his right arm and grips the defender's right sleeve with his left arm.

Right: this sequence shows how to escape from a scarf hold. The defender grips the attacker's jacket with both hands, makes a firm 'bridge' with his feet, shoulders and back, and breaks the attacker's balance. Even in floor fighting, balance plays an important part. Then the defender arches his body to his right and lifts his attacker away to the side . . . .

He continues to turn to his right, without loosening his grip

. . .

so that his attacker lands on his back and the defender is able to rise to his knees . . . .

He quickly climbs across the attacker's body, before the attacker can take any counter action, maintaining his grip to press his partner down . . .

then he assumes the same scarf hold, but on the opposite side of the body.

as a standard from which the real teaching and study of judo could begin. Japanese instructors were initially amazed at the regard given to black belt status, but eventually came to see it as a Western idiosyncrasy. It is true, however, that the black belt may only be worn at the end of a long period of training and grading examinations. To begin with a student may wear a red or white belt. The red belt may signify that as a beginner he is not only in the most danger but also the most dangerous. Between the red or white belts and the black belt there are yellow, orange, green, blue and brown belts. At each stage a student is expected to know more techniques and more theory of judo. He is graded by having to fight his peers and by demonstrating not only the techniques which belong to his particular grade but also any of the techniques he has learned before. For black belt status he must take a written examination as well, and in some clubs he must fight as many as ten of his peers in succession. The

Opposite page, above left and right: *the attacker raises his partner's arm, turning his hips in to the body, and with a combined action of bending forward and pulling on the captured arm performs a variation on the famous judo shoulder throw.*

Opposite page, below: *a demonstration of how to perform the hip throw.*
Above, left and right: *an outer reaping throw in which the leg is swept or 'reaped' from under the opponent.*

examining board is in general strict, since they wish to preserve the standards of their club or association. Altogether there are five grades of black belt which can be attained on technical merit and fighting ability, followed by further awards based on other aspects such as service to the art and research as well as skill. Although the grading system may vary from country to country and from association to association, this outline gives a good working notion of the general approach.

One of the European founding fathers of judo, E. J. Harrison, studied the art in Japan during the early years of this century. He tells how at that time it was required as part of the black belt examination to submit to strangulation into unconsciousness, followed by immediate resuscitation. This ritual is not part of the current judo system.

A high degree of fitness is necessary to practise good judo, but judo itself will make you very fit if you train regularly. Weights and other training aids, although used by many judo students, are not essential. If you wish to do judo merely for enjoyment, any good club will bring you up to the necessary standard. However, if you are in really poor shape do not start judo until you have done some regular jogging and other calisthenics. Some minor injuries can be expected in judo, but if you learn to fall correctly these will be limited to stubbed toes, bangs on the shin, and the occasional bruised elbow.

Some judo clubs advertise themselves as teaching judo for self-defence. This is totally misleading; you can become a highly skilful judo player and yet be poor at defending yourself. In judo there are rules. You know more or less what your partner may do. There is a mat between you and the floor, and the fighting area is open. There are no weapons. In real life there are no rules and your antagonist is a completely unknown quantity; the space may be cramped, with projecting obstacles, the floor concrete or littered with rubbish, and your attacker may be armed and dangerous. If you wish to learn self-defence, go to self-defence classes. However, if you want to learn about the fighting spirit and combat, and wish to acquire some new physical skills, go to judo.

AIKIDO

*A typical, spectacular aikido throw,
in which the person being thrown must
fall, due to the pressure on his wrist.*

A clear view of the type of wrist pressure cultivated in aikido.

Like all other Japanese martial arts ending in the syllable 'do', aiki-do is a system adapted from earlier combat or 'jutsu' forms, restructured into a training method with several facets. It is simultaneously a sport, an art, a moral discipline and a philosophy. Its founder, Morihei Uyeshiba, was a deeply religious man, a follower of Shinto, the national religion of Japan. He studied many styles of jujutsu, but it was from the 700-year-old Daito-ryu style that he found his main technical inspiration. From about 1917 to the late 1930s he developed his own system called aiki-jutsu, which emphasized the combative forms. Later, when the emphasis changed, he altered the name to aiki-do. Of the 2,664 techniques of aiki-jutsu, comparatively few are used in modern aikido training.

Uyeshiba was a man to whom his pupils attributed supernatural powers. Reports tell of his ability to read the minds of his pupils and to sense

Above: *a full-length view of the same type of wrist pressure which will lead to a throw or submission on the part of the defender.*

Below left: *in this technique a lock is applied against the wrist, and the left hand applies pressure just below the elbow.*
Below right: *a full-length view of the same lock, used to bring a partner down to his knees. Continued pressure will send him to the mat, face down.*

A wrist lock almost fully applied . . .

turning into a throw.

their actions before they moved; he was even said to have the capacity to move instantly, and invisibly, from one point to another – a feat which he declared was very bad for him as it 'shortened his life'. Whatever the truth of these claims, Uyeshiba was undoubtedly a very unusual person, and none of his successors inherited all of his traits. However, they developed the art in their own individual ways. Koichi Tohei followed the more spiritual lines of aikido, investigating the concept of 'ki' or universal energy. The aikido-ka (aikido student) aims to harmonize his ki with that of his opponent, rather than opposing it, thus leading him into a throw. Kenji Tomiki, a famous judo exponent, saw in aikido a useful contribution to education, and he formalized the art into a recognizable syllabus with combative sporting aspects which is still studied worldwide. The Tohei and Tomiki styles may be cited as the two poles of aikido, and between them exist other styles emphasizing many different aspects.

From the purely technical point of view, aikido is a throwing art. The participants do not use grips on the opponent's clothing, as in judo, but either 'push-strike' the opponent's body or grip his hand or arm. There is a prescribed way of moving into an attack, to be followed by a flowing, circular, harmonizing defence leading into a throw or lock. An attacker is not meant to resist the defensive

counter of his partner but to go with it, ending with a submission or a type of fall known as a breakfall.

The concept of the circle, either in its entirety or in part, plays a central role in both the theory and application of aikido. If a force is travelling in a straight line, and you wish to use this force to bring about the downfall of the person producing it, you use the circle. For example, if you grip your attacker's arm, and lead him away to his left in a curve, a centrifugal force develops. If you continue to lead him in ever-decreasing circles, the centrifugal force increases. Finally, you apply a twist of the wrist, the smallest circle. This suddenly releases all the force and your partner is thrown. In actual training, students never describe a full circle as the throw takes place before it is completed, but the fundamental notion is the same. Also, not one but many circles enter into a throw, each passing through different planes. This form of movement has a strong aesthetic appeal, so in an aikido class you may find people with many different reasons for studying the art, one of which is the sheer pleasure to be gained from moving about in this free flowing way, without giving a thought to the martial aspects.

The dress worn in aikido is either a complete judo uniform – trousers, jacket and belt – or a judo jacket and belt with the traditional martial

A wrist lock in a different direction . . .   *turning into a similar throw.*

arts black split skirt or hakama. The system of grading or examinations follows a similar path to that of judo, with variations.

The first period of training in aikido consists of learning how to breakfall safely, then the simplest throwing, stepping and locking methods are taught. Most people are familiar with the Japanese tradition of sitting on the floor, and some of the techniques of the art deal with fighting from this sitting or kneeling position, as well as 'knee walking', which is part of traditional Japanese etiquette. Knee walking indicates respect; it shows that you have no intention of taking up an attacking standing posture. Also, if a person is higher up the social scale than you are, you must not rise above them, compelling them to look up to you. Characteristically, the Japanese always found a way of circumventing a social limitation and many of their martial arts techniques involve fighting from the floor.

After the basics have been absorbed, an aikido class might move on to training with the wooden sword or bokken, and the short staff or jo. Teachers who have studied the jutsu aspects of the art may include techniques allied to their favourite weapon such as the naginata or halberd, or the spear. Still further up the ladder, students can learn how to deal with multiple attackers, a skill for which Uyeshiba was famous. To perform this well, your

awareness of distance, timing, motion and position must be well developed. If three people attack you, as soon as you grasp the first one your relationship with the other two changes. With one man down, and the second coming at you sideways, the third may be behind you. Your next move must blend with the incoming third attack so that you can deal with it. This requires split-second judgement and adaptation, and only comes with a freedom of spirit, mind and body which the founder said was the heart of aikido training.

Aikido is not a system of self-defence. Some of the earlier jutsu forms contain excellent fighting moves, but unless you can learn these or adapt aikido moves such as striking the jaw with the palm for use in self-defence, do not let anyone delude you into thinking that aikido is effective on the street. Its principal contribution in this respect might be the training in moving and avoiding an attack.

More than any other Japanese martial art, with the exception of ninjutsu (see page 70), aikido has become associated with stories that many people find hard to believe. This is partly due to Uyeshiba's unusual abilities and the inevitable embroidery of the facts. One of Uyeshiba's feats, attributed to his control of universal energy or ki, was to allow a line of strong men to try to push him over. They never succeeded. Koichi Tohei

Above left and right: *the man on the left has slipped past his partner, using specific aikido footwork, so that he can grip his shoulders from behind . . .*

and pull him down onto his back.
Below: *a throw beginning with a wrist lock. In aikido it is the convention not to resist such locks in training, but to 'go with the flow' and perform an appropriate breakfall.*

Top: *preparation for 'knee walking'.*
Above: *beginning a 'knee-walking' exercise.*

demonstrated the unbendable arm. This consisted of extending the arm, slightly bent, and challenging anyone to try to bend it further. By all accounts no-one could. Since the time that such things were made public, arguments have raged within the martial arts fraternities as to whether the feats were merely the application of mechanics or the mysterious ki. In a way the explanations are unimportant. The fact is that whatever the reasons behind them, such feats require a co-ordination which is difficult to achieve. It may be that whatever it was that Uyeshiba found died with him, and no amount of speculation will revive it.

In the minds of most of the followers of Uyeshiba, the idea of competitive aikido ran counter to the fundamental ideas. Nevertheless, the Tomiki system has become very popular in many parts of the world. The competitions in Tomiki aikido involve two people; the attacker uses a solid rubber tanto or dagger, which is thrust at the defender in a straight line. This is not meant to simulate a real situation, as a knife attack can come from any angle. It is merely meant to stimulate an evasive move followed by a counterattack which brings the knife-man down and disarms him. If the attacker scores a hit on his opponent he is awarded a point and continues to retain the knife; when he is defeated, the defender scores a point and takes over the knife. These competitions are the acid test of the defender's technique and his understanding of the principle of aikido. In all honesty it must be said that such competitions do not usually demonstrate either of these aspects to the best advantage. All too often they develop into scrimmages in which the attacker refuses to go down and the defender is desperately trying to make him change his mind.

A final word about the physical strength needed for aikido. It is frequently described as a soft and gentle art, and many women of delicate build are to be found in aikido schools. Indeed, if aikido is performed in the true spirit then excessive force is not necessary. There is, however, a great variation in the interpretation of this notion, both from club to club and from teacher to teacher, so beginners should shop around in search of a club which meets their requirements. Whatever type of training is chosen, students should be aware that strong and flexible wrists and strong forearms are desirable for aikido. Other prerequisites are healthy lungs and a good circulation system, to deal with the endless getting up from the judo mats which cushion the students' falls. Getting up from the floor is the most tiring aspect of aikido training. On the plus side, students soon begin to enjoy the rhythm and harmony of the flowing actions.

31

JUJUTSU

Opposite page: *the ritual bow must be performed in a prescribed manner. During every phase the student is not only mentally on the alert, but is also able to react physically. Hence in the first phase (**top left**) he is 'ready'. In the second phase (**top right**) he takes one step forward, looking forward. In the third phase (**centre left**) he begins to kneel, still alert and able to react. In the fourth phase (**centre right**) his kneeling action is almost complete. In the fifth phase (**below left**) he is kneeling but able, through training, to move in a split second. In the sixth phase (**below right**) he begins his bow. He begins with his left hand so that his right hand is free to draw a weapon, such as a sword, short sword or dagger.*

Below: *the bow is completed.*

Of all the Japanese martial arts, jujutsu – or jujitsu – contains the most variety, is the most amorphous and is the most lacking in centralized organization. It attracts the martial arts adventurer and dilettante, as well as the dedicated student.

What can you find in jujutsu? Almost everything! The chief reason for this is that unlike judo, aikido and karate, which all boasted a modern 'father' or figurehead, jujutsu has none. In nineteenth-century Japan there were dozens of jujutsu schools, each with its own distinctive variations on battlefield and empty-hand combat. Some of these died out and others have continued up to the present day. As martial arts became more and more popular in the West, jujutsu teachers of varying experience and ability, who had studied the art in Japan, opened up clubs all over the world. Training in jujutsu in its country of origin takes a long time. Few Western teachers were able to stay long enough in Japan to gain a teaching qualification from a particular school. Instead, they learned a variety of jujutsu techniques from different schools, sometimes mixing them with aikido, judo and karate techniques, producing what is now a recognized form of modern, synthesized jujutsu.

Today, the jujutsu techniques taught in any particular club depend on the training background of the instructor, and not on the school to which he belongs. In one club you might find training in swordsmanship, throwing techniques and kick boxing. In another you might find an aikido type of training combined with the use of the long staff

Opposite page, above left: students face each other, ready for training in a particular technique. Note that the feet are ready to push off from the floor.
Opposite page, above right: the student on the right rises to attack.
This page, above: in a flash the student on the left leaps to his feet and attacks with a punch.
Opposite page, centre left: the student on the right grips his partner's 'lapel', ready to punch.
Opposite page, centre right: the defender applies a wrist lock.
This page, centre: by turning to his right, the defender brings his partner down with pressure on the elbow joint.
Opposite page, below left: the attacker seizes his partner to strangle or choke him.
Opposite page, below right: the defender replies with an arm lock.
This page, left: he brings the attacker down with pressure on the joints.

or bo, plus some Okinawan weapons such as the nunchaku and sai. This variety need not give rise to concern. Many jujutsu clubs of this type have excellent training methods and facilities.

If, however, you are looking for a type of training that can be traced back to the samurai, you will have to seek out an instructor who has remained true to an authentic style or ryu, such as the one illustrated here. This jujutsu style belongs to the Ryoi-Shinto ryu and dates back to the seventeenth century. By all accounts it is rooted in the training imparted to Japanese martial arts students by Chen Tsu U, a Chinese Buddhist of the Ch'an (Zen) sect who was a retainer of the Japanese Lord of Owari. Chen Tsu U met Hichirouemon Masakatsu Fukono, a wandering samurai who taught the Ryoi-Shinto style of jujutsu, and introduced him to the Chinese version of the art. From this meeting it is said that a new approach to jujutsu began which eventually led to the creation of judo. The Ryoi-Shinto style has a definite syllabus of methods which include locking, throwing, striking, defending against weapons, arresting and tying up an enemy with rope, and the study of attacking the vital points of the body, atemi.

Atemi is an art common to all traditional jujutsu schools, and is based on experience in battle

This page, above: the attacker grips his partner prior to an attack.
Opposite page, above left: making use of his training in rising swiftly, the defender gets to his feet, turning left.
Opposite page, above right: he brings his attacker down and is ready to deliver a blow to the neck.
This page, centre: the attacker seizes his partner by his hair.
Opposite page, centre left: the defender rises, turning to his right; gripping his attacker's arm and hand, he raises the arm ready for the next phase of defence.
Opposite page, centre right: the attacker is pulled forward, his extended arm twisted and locked.
This page, right: the attacker seizes his partner by the throat.
Opposite page, below left: the defender rises swiftly onto one knee, drawing his attacker off balance, and turns into a shoulder lock.
Opposite page, below right: by bearing down on the shoulder of his attacker, the defender is able to lock him in a helpless position.

 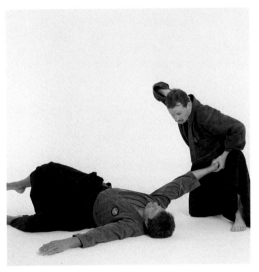

or one-to-one combat, and upon knowledge derived from acupuncture or similar healing methods. It was common for martial arts masters, both in Japan and elsewhere in the East, to combine a knowledge of taking life with a knowledge, however limited, of preserving it. Often a vital spot which under pressure produces intense pain, unconsciousness or death is precisely the spot at which to revive a person or alleviate pain. Rudimentary resuscitation techniques were known as kuatsu and are still taught in a few clubs. As we know from old scrolls and manuscripts, the Japanese were not averse to testing their famous swords and cutting skills on the bodies of condemned prisoners, and no doubt some of the more ardent jujutsu masters did not refrain from obtaining knowledge of atemi by a similar approach.

Within the many jujutsu training halls, therefore, there is something for everyone. No-one could sensibly aspire to learn all the techniques as they run into tens of thousands, but in a good club you would learn breakfalling, as in judo and aikido, throwing using locks as in aikido, and various jujutsu and judo throws including those that are banned from judo contests. You might also be able to learn sword techniques, but not kendo as such, the use of all or any of the Japanese–Okinawan weapons, plus variations of Thai and kick boxing. Some jujutsu schools specialize in self-defence, employing ancient techniques as well as modern methods culled from the Special Air Service (SAS) and various paramilitary and police forces. In their search for variety and synthesis, modern jujutsu teachers explore far and wide, borrowing ideas from the legendary ninja (see page 70) or from Western methods of wrestling.

A brief illustration will show the ingenuity and practical approach of jujutsu methods. Suppose someone comes up behind you and lifts you off the floor in a bear hug, his arms round your arms so that you cannot strike him over your shoulder or grip his groin area. What are you to do? You might try to drive your head back into his face, but he could avoid this. One suggestion is that you start to run. That is to say, you move your legs just as if you were making a 100-metre dash. Unless he is a giant body builder, your attacker will be unable to keep his grip. It is one thing to hold a relatively inert weight of 120–140 lb, but quite another to hold the same weight when it is running.

Within this wide arena of jujutsu an interesting phenomenon has arisen, echoing what took place in Japan over several centuries. Many teachers, finding themselves completely free to introduce whatever they wish into their own sylla-

Opposite page, top row: both men are in a 'ready' position, with the man on the right about to attack with a punch.
This page, top left: the attacker lunges at his partner's face.
This page, top right: the defender uses his palm to bring the punching arm down.
Opposite page, second row: the attacker follows up with a punch from the other hand, which the defender blocks.
Above left: the defender counters with a blow to the side of the neck.
Above: the attacker tries a third punching attack which is diverted by the defender.
Opposite page, left: the defender uses his palm to push his attacker's arm away and turn him to his left.
Left: the defender closes with his attacker.
Opposite page, below: the defender brings his right arm up under his attacker's jaw.
Below left: the attacker is thrown by the pressure on his jaw.
Below: the defender is poised to deliver a finishing blow with his right hand.

bus, have instead begun to specialize, sometimes finding a new side to the art, after years of study, which has attracted and held their attention. In such cases the foundations of a new, personal style are being laid. Take for instance the idea of using a small circle to produce a similar effect to that achieved in aikido using a big circle. In aikido the circles used to disturb and throw a partner are usually large, with big body movements. Suppose that you cut out the big body movements, can you manage the same result, i.e. the downfall of your partner? Some jujutsu enthusiasts have investigated this idea and have found that it works. All that is needed is a sharper, more intense action, producing more instant pain in the wrist or arm of a person and he will submit or be thrown.

This open approach of the jujutsu fraternity lends itself to discovery and rediscovery, but also has its dangers. These include the possibility of spreading training so widely and therefore so thinly that nothing is learned thoroughly. Beginners especially should watch out for this; if possible they should ask the teacher to help them master some basic techniques before exploring in new directions.

Before joining a jujutsu club, ask if you can watch a beginners training session. This will give you some idea of the atmosphere. Does the teacher seem to know what he is talking about, is he too hard on his students, is this the type of atmosphere that appeals to you? Once you have become a member of a club, keep an open but critical mind. Do not accept that a technique works simply because someone else says so; find out for yourself if it does. If a technique seems to depend entirely on your partner's willing co-operation, or if it is long and complicated, you can usually assume that it is not a true combat or jutsu technique, but belongs to the 'do' or art side of the syllabus. This important point can be illustrated. Some throwing techniques which are applied using a wristlock depend initially on the lock being applied successfully. The successful application of the lock depends on the wrist of the person who is to be thrown being relaxed and pliable. In a combat situation this opportunity almost never offers itself. The wrists of a fighting man or woman are usually firmly flexed if not quite tense. Your chances of seizing a wrist and locking it are virtually nil. So this means that these particular techniques can only be used in training. The reasoning behind their use is not difficult to follow. If we wish to explore as many wristlocking techniques as possible, then we will seize and bend the wrist in every available way. Having done this we will discover how many ways a particular lock can be applied to produce a throw. From such an investi-

gation some practical and swift techniques will emerge, while others will emerge as impractical but interesting to perform – more art than craft! Quite simply, the jutsu forms are a study in practicalities and the 'do' forms are a study in possibilities.

Modern jujutsu schools which train in 'do' forms are actually contradicting their name, but as the social conditions which gave rise to the original jujutsu schools no longer obtain, and we do not need to know what to do on the battlefield if our swords are swept from our hands by a charging horse, this point is no more than an intellectual one. On the whole the 'do' forms are more interesting in the long term and invite endless exploration.

Some martial artists, including jujutsu teachers, extend the study of their art to include physiological and mental aspects. Scientific medical research has shown that where movement is concerned different areas of the brain are involved in the learning process. In the initial stages of learning, while the cerebral cortex is building up new nerve pathways helped by what is called the pyramidal system, movements are gross and clumsy. Once all the other support systems such as the inner ear and the eyes have caught up with the instructions for the new movement, then the extra-pyramidal nerve system comes into play, refining the movements and sending the new information back to the cerebral cortex. Such information, however oversimplified, can enhance one's attitude to learning. The sooner an awareness of the finer movements and adjustments needed to learn a technique is developed, the quicker it can be learned. Research has shown that a part of the mid-brain known as the reticular system plays an important part in this process, sifting through the rain of sensory information sent to the cerebral cortex and deciding on the best way for the body to act.

Such knowledge introduced into the field of jujutsu and martial arts in general helps to enliven one's study and elevate combat into a true art form.

Opposite page: speed of action and finding the right opening is important in jujutsu, as in all martial arts.

*The donning of kendo armour
is part of the traditional ritual.*

KENDO

Kendo, a type of Japanese fencing, uses some of the classic techniques of real swordplay, and others that are peculiar to its sporting aspect. It is an exhilarating and dynamic art. The participants wear specially made light armour and the 'swords' used are made of four strips of bamboo held together with cord and soft leather. The helmet has a metal face mask. Of all the Japanese martial arts with a sporting element exported to the West, kendo retains the most traditional image. This is because it is affiliated with that symbol of Japanese craftsmanship, the sword. Some Japanese martial arts have climbed down from their traditional pedestal in the face of Western tastes and usage, but kendo has only given a slight polite bow. This is understandable when one remembers that the sword, the mirror and the jewel make up the imperial regalia of Japan. The sword is also found in religious shrines and some swords are priceless. Thus the image of kendo must not become tarnished.

Kendo as it is practised today dates back only to the late eighteenth century when the bamboo sword or shinai and the protective armour were introduced, allowing simulated combat to take place. From then on it went through a number of transformations, suffering near abolishment, then reviving to become part of the education of many Japanese boys and girls.

Part of the appeal of kendo to Westerners, although this may be denied by some practitioners, is the dressing up in armour. The jacket, or kendo-gi, is made of a heavy dark blue cotton, or white cotton criss-crossed by diamond pattern stitching. This stitching, apparently ornamental, has a practical use as it assists in the absorption of sweat and in the drying process. The hakama, a black split skirt made of many carefully pressed pleats, goes from

Left: a kendo student sitting quietly before a contest begins.
Above left: the two kendo students (kendo-ka) prepare for contest by taking up the correct posture with shinai touching, held just above the horizontal. Note the upright posture and whole attitude of attentiveness prior to the action.
Above right: the man on the right is first to attack, striking aside his opponent's shinai, or perhaps sliding his bamboo blade down the opposing blade.
Right: the final scoring movement takes place as the man on the right strikes his opponent's wrist, earning him a point.

waist to ankle and permits complete freedom of leg movement. The helmet, or 'men', consists of a metal grill with heavily stitched cotton flaps protecting the throat, the shoulders and the back of the head. Under the helmet a thin white cotton towel, often adorned with calligraphy, gives comfort and absorbs sweat. The gloves, or kote, are thickly padded and extend over the wrists. The waist and hips are protected by the tare, which is like a thick cotton belt with flaps hanging from it. The whole outfit is completed by the imposing breastplate, known as the 'do', which is also made of cotton but with the main section constructed from many strips of bamboo covered with leather to give firmness and protection to the chest.

The armour is put on in a special order and this underlines the highly ritualized nature of kendo. In a properly run dojo (training hall), the entire training session is planned according to the current kendo etiquette. People may not simply wander about talking and generally behaving as though they were at some informal social gathering. Bowing is taught from the beginning. One bows to the sensei (the teacher), to fellow pupils, and to the invisible ancestors and masters of the past and present.

Depending on the programme of the dojo, a beginner might first be taught how to hold a shinai and how to move the feet. There are certain definite ways of stepping which allow the body to be moved into an optimum position for carrying out a strike with maximum speed and efficiency. This basic way of stepping will be practised over and over again until it becomes second nature.

At the same time, the posture of the trunk and head is taught. This is a vertical posture. The hips, trunk and head are kept in line so that there is a smooth, unbroken movement forwards, sideways or backwards. As or when the basic movements become second nature, a variety of strikes and parries are taught. It is interesting to note that kendo techniques have developed along their own lines. Some of them would not be used in a real sword fight as they would be too dangerous for the attacker. This is not as strange as it appears, because kendo is a sport as well as an art, and in sport one performs techniques which one would not perform in real life. For instance, if you were to jump over a wall it is unlikely that you would do so using the same action as an Olympic high jumper. To learn real Japanese sword fighting one must study ken-jutsu or iaido (see page 48).

The mental side of kendo is just as important as the physical actions. Training in this aspect emphasizes the use of the eyes. Where one looks and how one looks can make the difference between victory and defeat. Some schools teach the practitioner to look at the opponent's eyes because, unless he has learned the art of keeping them 'neutral', they are likely to signal the coming of an attack. Other schools emphasize watching the tip of the shinai, or the hands, since the first actual movement will come from that region. Approaches to this vital question have varied. Miyamoto Musashi, the best-known Japanese swordsman and author of *The Book of Five Rings,* whose philosophy took Wall Street by storm some years ago, said that one should not bother with the outer appearance of the opponent; rather, one should penetrate into the eyes of his mind, to see his inner intention before he knows it himself. This level of awareness is not achieved in the early stages!

Other psychological aspects of kendo include achieving 'zanshin', which is difficult to translate but means something like having a clear, thought-free mind, and a determined, unshaking spirit. Through the teacher this combination of elements should be learned, so that it becomes possible to

Below: both kendo students assume the prescribed starting position.
Bottom left: the man on the left raises his shinai to make a cut to the head ('men'), holding the weapon directly above his own head in the characteristic position. Note how the elbows are thrown outwards. In the meantime his opponent has taken his own shinai into a diagonal position, having already decided on the different nature of his own cut.
Bottom right: both men attack, but the man on the right steps forward and to one side, avoiding the fully committed attack of his opponent, and cuts across the body, scoring a point by this recognized kendo blow.

prepare, attack, defend and finish an encounter with an unruffled inner state. To charge this stage with more energy, kendo-ka (kendo practitioners) use a particular shout, or kiai, uttered at the moment of attack. This kiai (from the Japanese *ki* meaning spirit, and *ai* meaning meeting) is widely used during contests.

As in most martial arts, the correctness of technique is of paramount importance in a kendo competition. To score, the strike must be accurate. There are only certain parts of the body which give scoring points. The sword or shinai must be used correctly, and a blow delivered with the side of the weapon's blade is not counted, since this would not in real life be a blow with the cutting edge. The competition follows strict rules intended to ensure that the competitors fight safely, in accordance with etiquette and in a spirit of mutual respect.

In addition, there is another side of kendo with a different emphasis. This is kata, a type of training using a wooden sword, usually made of oak, with a plastic or hide guard. Kata, also known as koryu kendo or 'old-style sword way', has been encouraged by the Japanese authorities to safeguard kendo from degenerating completely into a sport, where the scoring of points and the winning of tournaments eclipses everything else. In kata training the technical purity of the art is maintained; the absolutely correct use of the sword is learned, so the original combat source is not lost. This means that while in competition a student might attack from too distant or too close a position, in kata he learns the exact distance from which to launch an attack. He trains with a partner, without armour, and no blows actually touch the body. Foot positioning, posture, timing, correct attitude, breathing and all the aspects of good kendo appear in the kata. It exemplifies the Japanese preoccupation with order.

Kendo is a physically demanding martial art. It involves a lot of work for the shoulders and arms and this will be tiring until the muscles become accustomed to the effort. The rest of the body of a normally fit person should be able to cope with kendo training quite adequately.

Above left: the kendo-ka are ready to begin their contest.
Above right: here is an example of superior speed. The man on the right has raised his shinai swiftly and decisively, while his opponent has still not decided what course of action to take.
Above: still with the initiative, the man on the right leaps forward and strikes straight to the head ('men') of his opponent, scoring a recognized point. It is one of the rules of a kendo contest that as a kendo-ka makes his attack he must call out the name of the part of the body he is aiming at. Consequently, cries of 'men', 'do' and 'kote' echo constantly around the kendo training hall or dojo.

IAIDO

Two iaido students perform a kata together. Note the turn of the trunk, and the palm resting on the back of the blade. An imagined enemy is always in the mind's eye when performing a kata. Every movement has a purpose and must be correctly carried out to ensure the safety of the practitioner, as well as the downfall of the foe.

Iaido is an elite Japanese martial art which developed from training in sword combat techniques known as iaijutsu. The purpose of iaijutsu was to draw the sword and kill the enemy, preferably in a single action. There were many schools or ryu of iaijutsu, and some of the masters saw in sword training the possibility of developing the character of a man, as distinct from equipping him for battle. Nevertheless, the term iaido was not widely used until the twentieth century, when the art took its place among the other accepted forms of Japanese Budo, the Ways of the Warrior. This distinction does not mean that iaido is an ineffective fighting method; it is merely that the 'do' and jutsu sides of the art have a different emphasis.

Iron swords have been found in Japan dating back several centuries BC, but it was not until the

A sequence of kata movements demonstrating how to draw and sheath the sword. As these movements are carried out, the performer tries to maintain a state of 'zanshin', or thought-free concentration and awareness.

eighth century that what is now recognized as the Japanese sword or Nippon-to was forged, supposedly by a smith called Amakuni of Yamato province. The sword, carried by every warrior, came to be known as the soul of the samurai, and symbolized not only his capacity to cut down an enemy but also to cut down his own ego and remain fearless, loyal, honourable and sincere. Between the time of Amakuni and the banning of swords in the late nineteenth century more than 2,000 schools of kenjutsu or swordsmanship were founded. Iaido is a remnant of the iaijutsu techniques that were part of kenjutsu and is performed alone. Kendo (see page 42) is what remains of two-man combat training. Some schools of kenjutsu still exist but they are almost unknown outside Japan.

In 1967 the All-Japan Kendo Federation called together a group of expert swordsmen who drew up a series of iaido techniques. Later, the series was augmented and became a nationally recognized syllabus called Seitei Iaido. Each technique consists of four distinct actions: nukitsuke – drawing the sword from its scabbard; kiritsuke – cutting with the sword; chiburi – shaking blood from the blade; and noto – sheathing the sword.

Although the Seitei Iaido is likely in time to become the most widely studied arrangement of techniques, in Japan there are still schools of iaido and iaijutsu, such as the Katori Shinto Ryu and the Muso Shinden Ryu, where other techniques may be learned. Indeed, iaido associations the world over do their best to preserve as many of the old forms as they possibly can, but since the social conditions for swordplay no longer exist, this threatens to become an increasingly difficult aim.

For reasons of safety iaido dojo are among the most strictly regulated of all martial arts training halls. Students need to have a responsible attitude from the moment they enter a club. Beginners will probably be expected to have equipped themselves with a blunt-edged sword from a martial arts shop. 'Live' or sharp swords are used only by experienced students.

As a great deal of kneeling down and drawing the sword from a kneeling position takes place, the knees and ankles take most of the strain but soon get used to the movements. At the same time the shoulders will be built up by the constant cutting action. Some of the cuts in iaido are executed with one hand; others require two hands, especially if the cutting action involves more than one technique before the sword is resheathed.

Iaido students must show respect not only for the sword and for their fellow students and teachers, but also for the etiquette of the art. As the dojo is a theoretical battlefield, one must remain alert, keeping erect and maintaining a free right hand at all times so that a draw can be made at a split second's notice. The correct distance should always be maintained between oneself and others, and a keen observation of what is going on, and who comes in and goes out of the dojo, is also necessary. The emphasis on awareness blends with the technical demands of the art, as it is in this state of awareness that it should be practised.

At one time students at the Katori Shinto Ryu were obliged to sign an undertaking with their own blood that they would follow the teachings and rules of the school. Demands of this sort helped to ensure that the style was preserved inviolate for nearly five hundred years. In the late twentieth century one cannot hope to recapture the spirit of feudal Japan in one's daily life, but in the dojo at least one should learn to respect and remember it. The Katori Shinto Ryu was founded in the fifteenth century by Iizasa Choisai Ienao, a distinguished warrior who was never defeated. At the age of 60, he undertook to worship every day for one thousand days at a particular Shinto shrine. During this period he purified himself and trained strictly in martial arts. He was rewarded with a vision of a powerful deity who offered him a book of martial strategy, predicting that he would become 'a great teacher of all the swordsmen under the sun'. It was after this that he started his own school, and lived on to the age of 102. Since then it has been the custom for the eldest son of the family to act as the headmaster. The school offers training in many different martial arts, but outside Japan it is best known for its sword techniques. It is highly regarded by the Japanese government. Unlike many other martial arts organizations, the Katori Shinto Ryu professes not to want many students; if the numbers increased it would be impossible to teach all the students correctly and the style would suffer. Fortunately for those of us who cannot go to Japan and be accepted, the existence of the Seitei Iaido syllabus and other less strict dojo still make it possible to train.

Speed is essential in any martial art but in iaido it is said to be paramount, particularly when drawing and cutting; the sheathing of the sword can be done at a more leisurely pace. When using a 'live' blade, extreme caution must be exercised over the position of the left hand, since in drawing and sheathing it is held close to the mouth of the sheath and it is not unknown for careless people to lose one or more fingers. One of the reasons for speed on the draw and cut is to prevent the enemy from knowing how and where you are attacking. With a slow draw he can see what you are doing and counter.

*Two different cutting methods. The man on the left (**above and below**) demonstrates a two-handed cut which is common both in iaido and kendo. The man on the right (**above and below**) shows an unusual draw and single-handed cut, combined with a cross-over step which is not often seen.*

Ideally, a student should be able to choose a sword of a length and weight which suits his height, build and strength. In the days when the Japanese warriors fought with swords this was a big consideration, as your choice could make the difference between life and death. Today, however, the choice of swords is strictly limited by the supply available from manufacturers.

The clothing worn in iaido is the traditional hakama or split skirt, and a jacket not unlike a judo jacket but shorter in length and with shorter sleeves. Variations in clothing can be found and ceremonial outfits are worn for special occasions.

What may seem like minor details are vitally important to iaido students. For example, if the jacket sleeve is too long or too short it can impede the speed of the draw. Similarly, if the jacket does not fit correctly or is tied down too tightly, this will hinder the raising of the arms; if the sword is not held at the correct angle it will not cut correctly and might in real life be damaged; and if the feet are incorrectly placed, and the toes curled under in the wrong way, this can spoil the action of rising to your feet or moving forward. Iaido is undoubtedly an art for the perfectionist. If you do not welcome such detailed considerations – and there are many more – then it is not for you.

Nor is iaido for the squeamish. The sword is always directed at a specific target on the human body, such as a vital organ or an important blood vessel or joint. When any of the many techniques of the art are performed the swordsman has one of these targets in mind. His action may look beautiful, the gleaming blade zipping through the air, but it is more than a brilliant display: every movement is directed against an imaginary enemy who is

Below: this sequence demonstrates attacking movements, shaking 'blood' from the sword, and the sheathing of the sword. The imaginary blood is always shaken from the blade; if left on it would spoil the metal and might 'glue' the blade to the wooden sheath, hindering a subsequent rapid draw.

waiting, sword in hand, to strike him down first. Awareness of this helps to concentrate the mind of the student, and keeps his feet on the ground.

Although the samurai tested their swords and techniques on the bodies of condemned criminals, today's students use pieces of bamboo or tightly packed cylinders of straw. These 'targets' are fixed vertically to the floor and the iaido student trains at cutting cleanly through with one blow. Each cut passes through the straw, which in the mass is quite tough, at an angle of about 35 degrees. A poor cut or a cut which presents the cutting edge at an incorrect angle will not be effective. This shows the student that however thrilled he may be by his performance of a kata, and however impressed uninformed spectators may be, in real combat he would not be as formidable as he appears to be. The most difficult cut to perform is the rising, single-handed cut delivered backhand, i.e. rising from left to right for a right-handed person. When he is able to carry out each different cut singly, a student will train at delivering an unbroken series of cuts which gradually descend the straw target, at 15-centimetre intervals, finally reducing it to a mere stub.

The sword most frequently used in iaido is the katana, which is at least 60 centimetres long and has a slight curve. It is carried with the cutting edge upwards and is worn thrust through the sash. The samurai films shown in the West usually depict actors wearing the katana. The tachi blade is also longer than 60 centimetres but has a greater curve than the katana. It is worn cutting edge down, and hangs from straps made of metal or leather. Blades between 30 and 60 centimetres are called wakizashi, the curve and style being similar to the katana. Very often the katana and wakizashi are worn

together, reminding those who have studied kenjutsu of the famous swordsman Miyamoto Musashi, who developed his own system of fighting using two swords simultaneously. The two swords worn together are called 'long-short' or dai-sho. Blades less than 30 centimetres, daggers, are called tanto.

The vocabulary used in iaido is extensive, and learning it helps to supplement one's initial feeble awareness of what takes place in the course of performing the art. For instance, there is the sword point, the temper line, the ridge line of the blade, the cutting edge, and the back of the blade. These are all different surfaces which have different purposes. A simple example is the deflection by your blade of an attacking blade. This is never carried out by using the cutting edge as it would be damaged. Instead, the back or the side of the blade is used.

Iaido students learn how to examine and take care of their swords. One of the first things that happens when an uninitiated person draws a sword from its sheath is that he holds the blade with his fingers. This is a big mistake. Even the slightest contact between the natural oils and grease which lie on the surface of the cleanest skin will leave a mark on the metal of a quality blade. Similarly, you should not breathe on a blade as your breath will condense upon it. When cleaning a blade, a special type of oil should be used. There is a complete ritual and sequence to be followed in taking care of the sword, which a good iaido instructor will pass on to his students.

For many people, the appeal of iaido is that it is a kind of microcosm of Japanese traditional life in which every action is orchestrated, and every object has its place.

KYUDO

The archer is in the kai position, showing the correct form for the fully drawn bow.

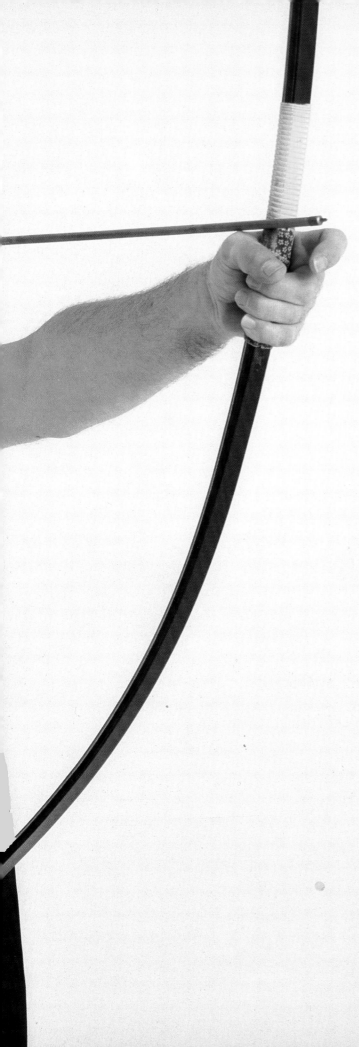

Kyudo means 'the way of the bow' in Japanese. In its purest form it is taught in conjunction with the study of Zen; without such study it is simply an external discipline, training in how to hit a target, for which the Western longbow is a much more effective choice of weapon. In kyudo, hitting the target or mato should be secondary to the state of mind of the archer or kyudo-ka. (The suffix 'ka' is used in most Japanese martial arts to denote the idea of 'he who trains' – i.e. a student.) Like kendo (see page 42) and iaido (see page 48), kyudo is an exercise in ritual. Unlike kendo, it is not a sport. A loose-fitting jacket similar to that used in aikido is worn and the traditional hakama or split skirt. The bow itself is very long; if one end is rested on the floor, the other rises above the head of the archer. The prescribed length of the arrows relates to the length of the outstretched arm of the student.

One of the first references to archery in Japanese history dates from the third century AD, when the pregnant Empress Jingo bound herself with bowstrings to ensure that her son would be strong and fit for war. This custom is still practised in parts of Japan. Kyudo is clearly a 'do' form, but originally it was called kyujutsu and was used in warfare. Dogs, confined in an enclosed space, were used for mounted target practise. The bow was sometimes used by the ninja (see page 70) because it was silent and could kill from afar. They also had a small version which could be concealed in their clothing. During the twelfth-century wars between the Minamoto and Taira clans, a leading Minamoto samurai, Tametono, had a bow almost three metres long which took three men to string it. In one battle Tametono fired the bow and such was the force of the weapon that the arrow passed through its first target and killed the man behind him. When Tametono was captured, the tendons of his arm were severed, putting an end to his prowess in archery. In 1170 he committed the first recorded act of ritual suicide or seppuku.

When the Portuguese introduced firearms into Japan in the sixteenth century, kyujutsu declined and the transformation into a 'do' form began. The Tokugawa era from 1603 to 1867 was much more peaceful than previous times and samurai and priests began to approach kyudo more in the way that it is approached at the present time. It is estimated that more than half a million people train at kyudo in Japan today, and in many other countries there is at least one dojo.

Top left: *standing at honza (the preparatory line), facing the mato or target. Omai, nakadachi and ochi describe the positions held by each archer.*

Top centre: *waiting in the kiza position (kneeling on upright feet) before performing rei (bowing).*

Top right: *turning away from the target, prior to preparing the kimono.*

Above and opposite page: *the uncovering of the left shoulder, and the tying up of the kimono by a woman with a tasuki (cord), prevents the garments from getting in the way of the string on release. It is also easier to see whether the correct muscles and lines of force are being applied on release.*

Opposite page, below centre: *facing the target.*

Opposite page, below right: *standing at sha-i (the shooting line).*

The physical act of preparing to shoot, drawing the arrow and bowstring, and releasing the arrow is divided into eight stages. The first stage, ashibumi, is preceded by a sequence of actions performed in the sitting position, which prepare the mind and body for what is to come. Ashibumi itself consists of setting the feet and legs into place. The next stage, dozukuri, involves putting the trunk and head into the correct position, as well as beginning to prepare the bow and arrow. Yugamae is the third stage, during which the arrow is nocked into the bowstring. The bow is raised during the uchiokoshi or fourth stage, and for the first time the kyudo-ka glances at the target. In the hikiwake or fifth stage, the bow is drawn using a special grip called the Mongolian lock, in which the string is held by the thumb. During the kai or sixth stage the student is calm and relaxed before he releases the arrow in the seventh stage, hanare. The final stage is called zanshin, a state of alert concentration when the kyudo-ka listens to the bowstring. It is said that a master can tell if a shot has been successful simply by listening to the string.

Success in kyudo does not mean hitting the centre of the target, however. Success, if that is the correct word, is the firing of the bow while being in the desired frame of mind. This state is one in which the archer is not driven by the wish to succeed. His mind should be empty of intention and filled with pure awareness of the present moment. This emphasis is why kyudo principally attracts those who have a strong feeling for ritual and tradition, combined with a desire to experience peaceful action. The paradox of releasing an arrow without being interested in hitting a target is related to Zen training.

This different attitude towards the target can be found on the other side of the Pacific Ocean among American Indian traditions. In Emmett Grogan's autobiographical novel *Ringolevio*, a

Top left and centre: *yatsugae –*
setting the haya or first arrow. The
feathers incline anticlockwise.

Top right: *yatsugae – setting the*
otoya or second arrow. The feathers
incline clockwise.

Above left: *uchiokoshi – raising the*
bow.

Above centre: *kai – the union of all*
the forces at full draw.

Above right: *hanare (the release) has*
occurred and the archer is in zanshin
(see iaido, page 48).

Pueblo Indian quotes a traditional hunting song:
'I aim my golden bow; I pull on my golden string;
I let fly my golden arrow; and it strikes the heart
of the target, and I fall dead. For I am the target.
And the target is me.' Just as the kyudo student
does not wish to think of the target as a separate,
external object which he must hit, so the Indian
senses that his prey is a part of himself. Both bow-
men feel that all life is inexplicably related.

Such an unusual discipline requires the constant attention of the teacher and kyudo dojo are
usually sparsely populated, both for reasons of space
and because the teacher cannot cope with dozens of
students at once. Japanese teachers traditionally
turn the newcomer away more than once. A student
must continue to 'knock on the door' several times
before being considered. The real reason for this is
that studying kyudo is a long and arduous process,
and the teacher does not want to start work with
someone who is going to give up after a short time.

He wants students who have a deep respect for the art, and who will carry on to the end. It is notoriously difficult to convince Japanese kyudo masters that Westerners can become dedicated to this psychologically taxing martial art.

Even though the hitting of the target is not the primary aim, it must not be thought that the physical technique is of no importance. J. S. Morisawa, an expert on the Chozen-ji school of kyudo, has written: 'You will never achieve realization of your true self-confidence if it is not created by your own hard work,' and 'pull the bow with determination to a point where you wonder whether your arm or the bow will break first.' Tens of thousands of arrows must be fired before the correct physical action is forged. This notion is clearly related to the Japanese belief that the attainment of black belt status in judo or karate means that a student can then be taught the true essence of the art, while Westerners think of this stage as a final goal.

While the body learns the physical technique of drawing, aiming and releasing, the breathing and mental training help to keep the mind free from ambition to score. In kyudo it is vital to breathe in a new way. Since breathing is a natural function, it is hard to understand the maxim that in kyudo one should 'breathe naturally', without forcing, when one is being given instructions about how this 'natural' breathing should take place. In kyudo training it is said that breathing should take place in the abdomen. This means that the passage of air into and out of the lungs should make itself felt in the lower trunk more than in the region of the rib cage. Advice is given to relax the muscles around the region of the solar plexus, to accommodate the 'swelling' movement of the lungs. This shift of attention aids the relaxing of the shoulders and chest. As the change in emphasis is brought about through relaxation and not through some kind of tension, it is referred to as 'natural'. Two results follow this change: a reduction in the frequency of breathing and a quieting of the nervous system. The total effect is to make the mind quiet also, a condition which is necessary for releasing the arrow without the intention of scoring.

When this key relationship between mind and body is right, the 'ki' or 'chi' will flow unrestrictedly and real meaning will be experienced directly, without the medium of any mental process. There is, however, a wide gulf between hearing about and experiencing such a state. Some kyudo schools teach zazen, or sitting in meditation. One must use the word 'meditation', because although purists would say that zazen simply means 'sitting', for outsiders the word is insufficient. In this context,

sitting is to sit, breathing 'naturally', with a silent mind which allows the chi to take its natural course. This sitting requires a rare vigilance. What is called enlightenment may come to someone engaged in sitting, but if he sits in order to become enlightened he will not experience it because his desire will block the way. This is analogous to the kyudo-ka releasing the arrow with no intention of hitting the target and helps to explain the practice of zazen combined with kyudo.

Very few people can simply be told about such things as zazen and immediately practise them, so kyudo teachers sometimes introduce a number of exercises or supplementary practices which lead a student towards the ideal. For example, there is the special walk, known in the Chozen-ji school as hojo. The student stands with his hands on his hips, his palms resting on his abdomen. He then walks in a straight line, sliding his feet rather than picking them up, and breathing in time with his steps. The trunk and head are kept vertical. This simple action is not as physically passive as zazen nor as active as firing a bow, but it has elements of both and can be seen as a kind of preparation. The Chozen-ji school also uses breathing exercises combined with simple body movements which are the same as qigong forms (see page 137). If a student finds that his mind wanders during any of these exercises, he is advised to count his breaths to give the mind something extra to focus upon. Even more assistance can be given to the quieting process by engaging in the art of calligraphy. Japanese and Chinese brush masters also use zazen and kindred forms to produce their beautiful brush strokes. For instance, some schools advise the student to inhale on lifting the brush and to exhale on making the stroke.

In all the diversity of physical action seen in martial arts there is a certain unity which is based on the search for a quiet and empty mind, or mushin. In the Eastern countries whose martial arts are outlined in this book, many of the actions of daily life, such as making tea, greeting guests, cooking and taking care of the body, have some type of ritualized forms. It is more than likely that the origins of these forms had something to do with bringing people closer to the spiritual potential inherent in them. As we in the West have witnessed the disintegration of most of our codes of behaviour and old customs, many of us have felt drawn to Eastern ways. To interested observers this presents a paradox. Why abandon with one hand what the other hand is reaching out for? Is it because we feel that the customs we are leaving behind are saturated with our frantic materialism, while the customs of the East are much less tainted?

RYUKYU KOBUJUTSU

The weapons of Okinawa comprise a formidable arsenal. Instead of beating their swords into ploughshares, the Okinawans, conquered and disarmed by the Japanese in 1609, turned their farming implements into weapons. The best known of these is the nunchaku, made famous by the ubiquitous Bruce Lee in his film *Enter the Dragon*. It consists of two octagonal pieces of wood connected by a doubled cord, and is said to have been developed from a rice or corn flail. The most distinguishing feature of such an implement is that it can deliver a powerful blow without its impact being felt by the user, since the cord cuts off the force from his hand without diminishing it.

Also well known in the West today, to all those who watch American police movies, is the tonfa. This came from the handle of the millstone used for husking rice. It is a heavy piece of wood, a little longer than a man's forearm, with a handle at one end at right angles to the main section. Police forces around the world, but particularly in the United States, have adopted a modified version of this weapon and have their own 'peace keeping' methods of using it. It is worn in a special holster at the hip.

The sai is a kind of fork-dagger. The handle and blade are made of one piece of metal, the blade being round or octagonal in section. Two distinctive prongs curve outwards from either side of the blade. The kama is a sickle with a long, straight handle and curved blade. In addition to these rural adaptations there is the paddle, the steel knuckle-duster, the 2-metre staff, the short-handled spear reminiscent of the Zulu assegai and the beautiful tortoiseshell shield.

The conquest of Okinawa was carried out by the Satsuma clan of southern Japan. Defeated in the great civil war of 1600 by the Tokugawa clan, they were sent to Okinawa to keep them out of trouble at home, where they endlessly plotted to overthrow the government. The inhabitants of the 1,125-kilometre island chain which is Okinawa, south of Japan and east of China, had refused to supply the Japanese with goods needed for their unsuccessful invasion of China in 1592, and the punishment was long overdue. As soon as Okinawa had been conquered, the Japanese leader Iehisa Shimazu decreed that the possession or carrying of weapons was forbidden. The reaction of the Okinawans was to develop fighting methods which did not involve the use of weapons. Imported at different times from China and Southeast Asia, these methods evolved into several indigenous systems known collectively as 'te' or

Opposite page: a student demonstrates a typical posture using the Okinawan paddle or eiku. This little-known weapon has given rise to few techniques but is very effective.
Below: the power and momentum of the nunchaku or rice flail is clearly shown as the student swings the weapon overhead, then round in a circle, finally catching it again. It is now under control and ready to be used once more.

hand, the forerunner of kara-te, meaning 'empty hand'. The Okinawans also began to train with the improvised weapons that they made from farming implements. Again they were influenced at first by Chinese and Southeast Asian 'models', but with characteristic resourcefulness soon adapted these models to their own requirements and temperament. Over the succeeding centuries the use of these weapons and of 'te' was improved and modified, different schools emerged, and as interest in karate grew in the West, so did the desire to become proficient in the art of the Okinawan weapons.

NUNCHAKU

Only one man stood between the luckless prisoners and death – Bruce Lee. Armed with his specially made nunchaku, cooing like a malevolent banshee, seeing everything but focusing on nothing, the hero of *Enter the Dragon* zapped the villains with equally dispassionate blows, sometimes felling two of them at a time. Audiences were inspired by this dynamic triumph of good over evil, and the nunchaku became all the rage for several years. Some American states and several European countries banned its manufacture, sale and use, overlooking the fact that the more you try to suppress something the more attractive it becomes. Western experts in nunchaku use bemoaned the fact that the weapon was acquiring a bad name with the police and juvenile courts.

Today, the hue and cry and the craze for nunchaku have died down. The essential weapon, without the sensationalism, has taken its place once more solely as part of the Ryukyu kobujutsu armoury. Ryukyu, meaning 'a rope in the offing', is the native name for Okinawa, while kobujutsu or kobudo refers to weapons used for combat, 'ko'

meaning ancient and 'bu' meaning war. The distinction between 'do' and 'jutsu' forms is explained in the section on aikido (see page 24). As in escrima (see page 150), the weapon use in kobujutsu parallels the empty-hand techniques, and several of the Okinawan weapons have equivalents elsewhere. For example, there are numerous Chinese versions of the nunchaku, one of which is the three-sectional staff used in wushu of China (see page 132).

Within the Okinawan martial arts systems different versions exist, one of the most popular being the Ryukyu kobujutsu of Shinken Taira, illustrated here. Earlier this century Shinken Taira took his system to Japan and bequeathed it to the present grandmaster, Inoue Motokatsu. One of the chief European exponents of this system is Julian Mead, resident in England.

According to Inoue, Shinken Taira was 'probably the greatest weapons genius of his time'. A man of unbelievable strength and will, at the age of 73 he would regularly travel from Okinawa to Japan carrying 20 long staffs, ten sai and a rucksack, for the sake of transmitting his art. Inoue himself is scarcely less formidable. There is hardly any Japanese martial art which he has not studied to a high degree of proficiency. Coming from a noble Japanese family, his first teacher was the fourteenth grandmaster of the Koga Ninja Ryu, Seiko Fujita, who also acted as bodyguard to Inoue's father. Amid the wealth of martial arts that he studied, the heir of Shinken Taira has preserved the kobujutsu system intact.

The nunchaku, sometimes tipped with metal, is primarily a striking weapon. The spectacular movements of Bruce Lee and the modified form of modern nunchaku combat have no place in what is principally a down-to-earth, practical system of fighting. The nunchaku can be used at long, medium and close range, and is sometimes swung in a figure of eight when advancing to attack. It can also be used for blocking and trapping the hands of an adversary. As it is a jutsu form, it cannot be used in any realistically simulated combat competition

as the risks are too great.

One of the biggest difficulties for the faint-hearted in learning this weapon's use is that the beginner usually hits himself several times before acquiring proficiency. To soften this process one can buy various foam-covered and even hollow plastic nunchaku. As one of the dictums of kobu-jutsu is 'learn from your bruises', it would be better to keep such items away from the training dojo as they would probably be frowned on by most sensei or teachers.

In the Ryukyu kobujutsu grading syllabus the nunchaku is not introduced until the fourth grade or second kyu level. (Kyu refers to beginner grades leading up to the black belt standard. First kyu is the highest beginners grade, and fifth kyu the lowest.) As with all Japanese bujutsu styles, the weapons of Okinawa have kata or pre-arranged sequences of movement which the student learns progressively.

TONFA

The millstone used for grinding on all Okinawan farms had a handle inserted into it which, when removed from the millstone, became a dangerous weapon. This tonfa or tui-fa is generally used in pairs – one in each hand – for simultaneous attack with both weapons or simultaneous defence and attack. The tonfa has not gained anything like the popularity of the nunchaku, but herein lies a distinction between the enthusiast and the dedicated student. The latter is not swept up by the excitement surrounding such personalities as Bruce Lee or one of his successors in the 1980s, Jackie Chan, but is interested in studying and preserving the complete system. To that end he endeavours to give as much time to one weapon as he does to another, even though he may have a marked preference.

The tonfa can be used in training against the other weapons of the system as well as against the sword, jo or staff and so forth. It is customary for kobujutsu students to study karate at the same time,

as many of the empty-hand movements are more or less the same as the weapons movements. An example of this is the rising block used in karate (see page 6). A rising arm, with clenched fist, could just as easily rise holding a tonfa, with the 'blade' lying along the forearm, extending the reach of the arm and protecting it from the impact of a fist or weapon. The end of the tonfa which protrudes from the fist is used for punching, and with the development of the required dexterity the blade can be swung in a circle from the hand to give a powerful strike, sideways.

This weapon is introduced at the third level of the Ryukyu kobujutsu syllabus for the third kyu qualification.

SAI

A pair of gleaming sai, wielded by an expert, thrills any audience at a martial arts demonstration. Although the sai has been described as a vicious weapon by at least one dedicated martial arts writer, this emotive expression need not detract from its appeal. Versions of the weapon are found in China, India, Southeast Asia and Japan, but it is the kobu-jutsu sai that has become famous. Nowadays made of steel, it is between 37 and 50 centimetres long and tapers slightly from pommel to point. The curved guard, making two sharp prongs on either side of the blade, can be used for trapping and turning a weapon or wrist.

Although it looks like a thrusting weapon, the sai is primarily for hitting and blocking; thrusting techniques are not ruled out, however. Mainly used in pairs, it can sometimes be seen in threes: one in each hand and one thrust into the belt, perhaps for throwing, like a knife.

The sai is introduced at the second level of the kobujutsu syllabus for the fourth kyu grade.

KAMA

Just as only the more experienced students of iaido

Opposite page, top: a strong blocking movement using the nunchaku to defend the face.
Left: a pair of tonfas being used as defensive weapons. Note the firm hold and strong stance , covering the head and lower trunk.
Above right: a typical forward striking action using the sai.
Centre right: using two sai to block an attack and simultaneously counter with a strike to the head.
Right: here the two sai are used in different positions, but with equal effect, to defend and counterattack simultaneously.

A block and counter (top), using one tonfa. Many of the techniques of the tonfa (centre) and kama (bottom) are interchangeable. The weapon in the right hand is used to

block and catch the staff, sweeping it in a big circle to the right. The weapon in the left hand is used to make a counterattack.

(see page 48) are allowed to use live, sharp blades in training, the kobujutsu student has to wait until the fifth grade before he is permitted to train in techniques of the live sickle or kama. If a kama expert managed to get close to an enemy, the latter's death was certain, as this is possibly the most difficult weapon of all to counter, especially when used in pairs. The razor-sharp blades, curving in from two different angles, present an almost insurmountable problem. There is no weapon technique that is beyond the capabilities of the kama: it can slice, chop, stab, block and hook in any situation. The utmost care must be exercised when learning to use this weapon.

The sickle shape has been used on other weapons such as the spear, where a crescent-shaped blade was fixed at the end of a long handle, at right angles to it, or combined at a different angle with a hooked or pointed weapon. These variations were invented by Japanese warriors, and used by the samurai and warrior priests.

Another version of the kama itself was used in feudal Japan. This was the kusarigama (kusari-kama) which consisted of a kama with a metal handguard in the form of a right-angled loop, and a chain attached to the point where the blade was fixed onto the handle. A light weight was often joined to the free end of the chain and was used for striking an enemy before moving in for the kill with the blade, or for skilfully wrapping round a weapon, limb or neck, to trap or entangle. The ninja (see page 70) were skilled in the use of kusarigama, as were other famous warriors. The blade of this kama was double-edged and was used for chopping off heads. The chijiriki is a variation of the kusarigama, consisting of a long staff with a ball and chain swinging from it. The manrikigusari is a chain weighted at both ends. It was invented by Masaki Toshimitsu who was a guard at the main gate of Edo (the ancient name for Tokyo). This gate was considered a holy place and the chain was devised as a weapon that could be used without any blood being shed in hallowed precincts. The question of the violence itself must have been secondary. This weapon is reminiscent of the whip, the lasso or the South American bolas; in fact, in modern times, for the sake of safety in training, a rope has replaced the chain and the weights are lighter than those used originally.

Learning about the use of weapons of this sort inevitably raises in one's mind the question of whether or not such arts should be taught today in an increasingly violent world. At the present time the British Parliament is considering passing a bill that would make it a criminal offence to use some of the martial arts weapons. They have, however, come across certain logistical problems. Dozens of ordinary objects, such as monkey wrenches, carving knives, scissors and walking sticks, can become lethal weapons in the hands of someone intent on doing harm or a rape victim desperately trying to defend herself. Chinese kung fu even includes the art of fighting with a small bench! Indeed, the existence of kobujutsu itself demonstrates how an artisan's tools can be turned into weapons of war. The original Chinese written characters for martial arts or wushu depicted the action of 'stopping or preventing fighting', and it is in this light that all martial arts should be viewed.

TIMBE AND ROCHIN
The tortoiseshell shield or timbe and the short spear or rochin are used together. The shield often has a small spyhole in the centre for viewing the enemy. Some commentators equate the short spear with an agricultural implement which could be stuck into the rice plant to carry it. On the end of the spear there is a short tassel which some people believe was used as a means of holding on to the weapon if the wooden handle was knocked out of the hand. The combined use of the timbe and rochin is unique to kobujutsu of Okinawa.

EIKU
The Okinawan paddle's use is so obscure that it would have probably died out had it not been for the continued support of Grandmaster Inoue. Blocking, striking and thrusting are all possible with this weapon, but one of its more imaginative uses, which appears in the only eiku kata, is the flicking of sand into an opponent's eyes, temporarily blinding

Below: a typical stance displaying the use of the timbe or shield, and the rochin or short spear. The one-legged position comes from raising the leg to avoid a sword or staff blow, while the rochin strikes down to counterattack.

him. Sometimes the wide end of the paddle was tipped with metal.

TEKKO

The tekko or knuckle-duster has been used for centuries, in both the East and the West, to protect the hand and increase the impact of a punch. The Okinawan version is made of solid metal and fits the hand like the proverbial glove. In India a spiked version is known; in Thailand a glove laced with broken glass or other sharp material was once used in boxing bouts; and the thugs of the Western world have not been averse to using various versions. In

World War I knuckle-dusters were sometimes used in combat, and in our ingenious modern times the wallet knife, a short blade held so as to protrude from the fingers, found its way onto the market a few years ago. Tekko use is taught only at black belt level in kobujutsu.

BO

Finally, there is the 2-metre staff, one of the most widely used weapons both in Okinawa and Japan. Its full name is rokushakubo – in Japanese the word 'roku' means six, the word 'shaku' is a measure of length – approximately 30 centimetres – and 'bo' means pole or staff. The bo varies in shape, but the kobujutsu version tapers from the middle to the ends.

In kobujutsu the bo is the first weapon to be taught, as it is in some ways the most demanding, versatile and clearly related to empty-hand methods. New techniques are introduced at every level of the kobujutsu syllabus and as there are no

Above left: the man on the left raises his staff or bo to deliver an overhead strike, but . . .
Left: the man on the right delivers a thrusting attack to the neck before he can complete it.
Above: a student takes up a fighting stance, wearing the knuckle-duster or tekko.

fewer than 22 basic and nine advanced bo kata, the study of the bo can be a lifetime's work. Certainly a student must train for several years before an acceptable standard is reached.

The Japanese bo, which is more frequently made without the taper, allows the use of heavy, head-on blocks, whereas anyone using the kobujutsu bo must rely on deflections and rapid counter-attacks. As one would imagine, a 2-metre staff gives its user a big advantage in many circumstances, but close up he becomes just as vulnerable as anyone else.

The widespread availability of staffs and sticks in an agriculturally active country such as Japan or its less well-known neighbour Okinawa, meant that many people could resort to its use in an emergency. The seventeenth-century Japanese poet, Basho, was an adept user of the bo, and many hermits, monks and travellers carried one, not only for protection but also to assist them over rough ground, and they could even suspend their baggage from it. Sometimes the bo was bound in metal to give more weight and durability when used against a metal weapon. Another advantage the bo had compared with other weapons is that a lower level of skill than that needed, for example, to use a sword correctly, could make it effective. Blocking or thrusting, sweeping or striking, the sheer size and momentum of the object stamped a certain authority on even the most basic technique.

The renowned Katori Shinto Ryu respected the bo sufficiently to include it in its syllabus. Students perform the bo kata against a swordsman. Of the 316 known schools of bo which have appeared in Japan's history, the Katori Shinto Ryu style is one of the most effective and compares favourably with that of Ryukyu kobujutsu. However, it is distinct from the latter in that it has deeper cultural and religious roots. Like many other nations, the Japanese have a tradition of 'mudra' or hand positions, seen on Buddhist and Hindu statues, which have a specific psychological meaning. The Katori Shinto Ryu tradition has a number of these mudra, the inner meaning of which is secret, although their external form is known. The school's grandmaster, Risuke Otake, states that one of the purposes of the mudra is to induce a state of 'self-oblivion' or lack of concern for the ego. As each sign is made, a number of specific syllables are chanted; originally this was to help the warrior free himself from personal considerations and fears as he went into battle or single combat. Such information underlines the depth of martial arts study, removing it from the sphere of mere superficial violence.

NINJUTSU AND SHURIKEN-DO

Two ninja in typically alert positions.
Opposite page: *kuji-kiri, secret hand positions used by the ninja to evoke inner forces.*

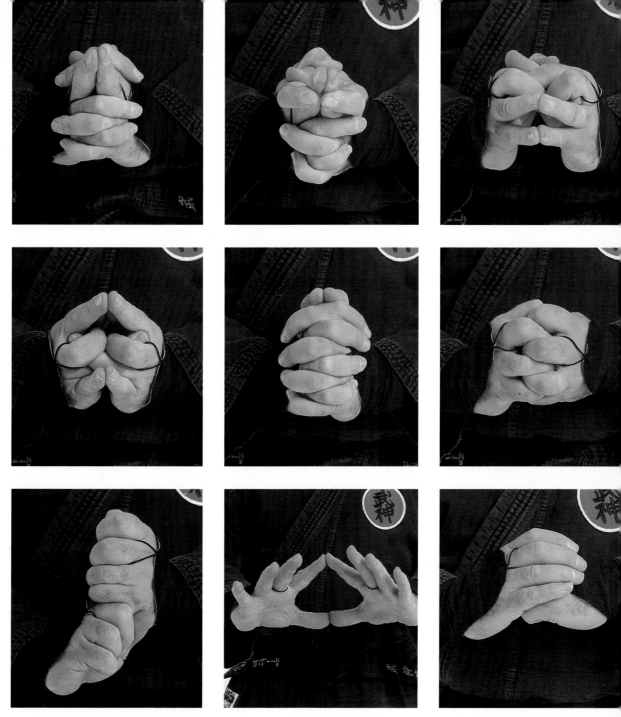

The hooded shadow warriors or ninja, the men of stealth, have captured the imagination of many Westerners since they appeared in the James Bond film *You Only Live Twice*. Not surprisingly, their background is obscure. The very nature of such people's work – as spies, assassins, secret agents – precludes the keeping of careful records since their success depends upon remaining unknown. Men who reputedly bit off their tongues and bled to death in captivity rather than submit to torture and possible revelation could hardly be chosen as allies of the historian. Such were the ninja, the men of ninjutsu. Masters of disguise who cultivated the skill of becoming almost invisible, they were the phantoms of Japanese military life.

In recent years ninjutsu has made a complete volte-face under the leadership of Dr Masaaki Hatsumi and his best-known Western pupil, Stephen Hayes. The ninja are now presented as men and women who try to help one another and society. Students are encouraged to use their knowledge and training to become better citizens, so one cannot really say that the new ninja are the true heirs of their ancestors. Modern ninjutsu has a humanitarian face and an appeal to brotherhood. Ninja students are known to one another and have no desire to create a secret society.

The scanty history that does exist is based on fact, conjecture, hearsay and legend, and places the beginnings of ninjutsu between 500 and 300 BC. Although considered to be a Japanese art, it appears to have been Chinese in origin, many of the ele-

ments of ninja techniques being found in the famous treatise of General Sun Tzu called *The Art of War*, written in about 400 BC and said to have been a source book for Mao Tse-tung and many other less significant revolutionary fighters. To appear, harass the enemy, then melt into obscurity as this book advises became a favourite ninja tactic. Within the framework of this tactic there are many detailed requirements: one must remain concealed, attack without warning, escape and hide. The ninja needed an all-round knowledge of people, places, terrain, human weakness, medicine, poison, and as many weapons as they could find, invent or improvise.

According to some sources the first notable use of the ninja dates back to the time of the Japanese regent, Prince Shotoku, AD 574–622. Groups of warrior priests, yamabushi, rebelled against the Imperial forces and the ninja were employed to seek them out and destroy them in their mountain strongholds. However, some modern writers state that the ninja originated from the warrior priests themselves. In time around 25 ninja guilds or schools were established, and in some parts of Japan they provided a second unofficial 'government', ruling by terror and assassination. On rare occasions the ninja were involved as an elite force in pitched battles. Their last major engagement took place in 1673 during the Shimabara wars, when they fought against 40,000 Christians on the island of Kyushu.

In addition to their strict code of silence, expediency seems to have been a prominent trait of the ninja. They hired themselves out to anyone who could afford their services. The Koga ninja, named after the province where they lived, were particularly active on behalf of the Tokugawa clan who came to power in Japan in the seventeeth century, but their allegiance to the rulers did not prevent them from being of service to much more lowly employers such as merchants.

Above left: the beginning of a kata, showing a form of stepping peculiar to ninjutsu. Hands and feet are wide apart.
Above centre: the hands are brought down and the feet cross over.
Above right: the original stance is resumed, with the head turned to the left.
Opposite page, above left: the man on the left tries a ninjutsu lunging punch.
Opposite page, above right: using the formal stepping technique, the man on the left moves out of the line of attack, to counterattack.
Opposite page, below: a display of traditional ninja weapons, many of which are now banned in most European countries and in many parts of the United States.

The ninja clans lived in close-knit communities. The hierarchy consisted of leaders or jo-nin, sub-leaders or chu-nin, and men who carried out the operations on the ground, ge-nin. (The prefixes jo, chu and ge, meaning upper, middle and lower, are used in many martial arts styles to designate target areas on the body.) Secrecy was paramount and the revealing of clan secrets to an outsider, or even to an uninitiated member of the same family, was punishable by death. This underlines the contradiction inherent in the modern scene, where ninjutsu is taught openly to all.

If captured, a ninja would try to commit suicide in any way that he could. If he were unwilling or unable to kill himself, a fellow ninja would try to find a way to bring about the same result, perhaps by the use of poison. Technique, lore and discipline were traditionally passed on from father to son. Scrolls outlining these codes of practice were family treasures, but in modern times many have become collectors' items.

Dr Hatsumi, the smiling and mild-mannered father of modern ninjutsu, is reputed to have many valuable scrolls. Controversy may still be heard concerning Hatsumi's ninja lineage, but he shrugs it off. As far as the martial arts world is concerned he is the grandmaster of ninjutsu. People from all

over the world have made the pilgrimage to his dojo in Japan, to gain more knowledge and drink in the unique atmosphere of the place. One of the features of his retreat is a ninja museum where many items from the past are on display.

Hatsumi's martial arts career began in a dramatic way. His father was an alcoholic and in his cups would brandish a knife in the home. As a young boy Hatsumi would run and hide, but he remembers being able to recognize the state his father was in before he entered the house, hearing the different rhythm of his footsteps from afar. As he got older, he learned martial arts in order to be able to control his father and put him to bed. Hatsumi's ninjutsu teacher was Toshitsugu Takamatsu, a fearsome man who had spent years in China where he earned the name Mongolian Tiger. Takamatsu lived to be an old man and laughingly attributed his longevity to having transformed himself into a house cat, from a Mongolian Tiger. 'Everyone knows how much women like to cuddle house cats in their laps,' he said. Hatsumi described his teacher as awesome, and found it hard to believe that a man living in the modern world could have such an aura of feudal power.

A hint of the type of training that Hatsumi received from Takamatsu throws light on the traditional ninja outlook. The samurai sword is razor sharp. Takamatsu once drew a sword and told Hatsumi to grab it. At first the student thought his master was joking; he was not. With the sort of faith that few can muster, Hatsumi grabbed the blade without further hesitation. He was not cut. The master also tested him by stealing silently up behind him and delivering a sword cut. Hatsumi sensed something and flattened himself on the floor. This test remains in the ninjutsu syllabus for grading at the higher levels of training. One must have unshakeable confidence in oneself and in the teacher. Many Western students fail this test.

Hatsumi was taught everything that Takamatsu knew, and also absorbed his spiritual values and humanitarian view of life. During a tour of the West some years ago he explained to a large gathering of students, who had just finished a training session, that he was dismayed by the turn ninjutsu training had taken outside Japan. To many people the realm of the ninja is one of fantasy, bordering on science fiction. Hundreds if not thousands of students have been 'conned', to use Hatsumi's word, by bogus instructors. Others argued like spoiled children about who was the better ninja. He urged the students to grow up and leave behind juvenile ideas about the art.

Distorted ideas about the ninja have been

Top right: *the man on the right lowers his body and slides his right foot forward, to avoid a punch and prepare a counterattack.*
Centre: *he presses down to bring his shin into contact with that of his attacker.*
Above: *continued pressure and forward movement forces the man on the left to fall, leaving him wide open to attack.*

Top: *the man on the right avoids an attack and takes hold of his attacker's right arm.*
Centre: *securing a wrist lock, he turns his attacker to the left.*
Above: *one of several postures for throwing the shuriken or star.*

stimulated by the media, who have exploited the image of the shadow warriors in their black garb and menacing hoods. Men who can leap 6 metres in the air and appear and disappear through apparently solid walls never existed, except on 16 millimetre film and the printed page. Today's youth, hungry to latch on to such beguiling fantasies, were all too easily carried away by a barrage of images from what has become a sub-culture within our society, the ninja film. Hatsumi told his students that as well as learning to deal with the enemy without, they must struggle with the naive enemy within.

Modern ninjutsu training is done on a hierarchical basis with different awards marking a student's progress. The basics include kicking techniques, learning to break one's fall, perform long-range punches, walk in specific ways, and to relax as much as possible. A high level of all-round fitness is required.

One of the common effects of much Japanese martial arts training in the West is to produce too much tension in students. This is partly because the early Japanese teachers issued their commands in military style. Few new recruits to a dojo could remain relaxed when screamed at from a distance of a few metres. Within minutes, they were all sweating as much from nervous tension as physical effort. Hatsumi's approach is different. He wants ninjutsu students to learn to motivate themselves, developing their own abilities and relying on their own common sense, rather than being driven into action by a martinet. In some ways this puts more of a burden on the student than the parade-ground approach, as most people who decide to learn a martial art want to be taught. Much of the Western educational system consists of learning by rote, rather than using one's own initiative, and it takes time to learn how to teach oneself from what one is taught.

One item of ninja clothing is particularly unusual. This is the tabbi or soft boot, which divides the big toe from the other toes, providing a useful gap that makes climbing easier. Black, heavy-duty uniforms are worn, similar to those used in karate but with special cotton 'gaiters' round the legs and extended sleeves that cover pale hands at night. The famous ninja hoods, now hardly ever used, were also worn at night, so all that could be seen of these stealthy secret agents were the whites of their eyes.

The weapons and tools of the ninja's trade are many and varied. They include a short staff or hanbo, metal claws for climbing and defence, chains weighted at one end, and powder that can be blown into an enemy's eyes to put him tempor-

Top row: *an attempted attack by the man on the right is met by a strike to the head, followed by a wrist lock and (**bottom row**) a powerful turn which brings the attacker down.*

arily out of action. The ninjutsu student also studies most of the recognized weapons of the Japanese martial arts systems, although the favourite sword of the ninja is straight and not curved like that of the samurai. Many techniques similar to jujutsu (see page 32) are also learned, and given the name taijutsu. Tai means body, so taijutsu means body-combat art; in this system the body as a whole is regarded as a weapon, and anything it can do

to preserve itself is legitimate. Ninjutsu has no limitations.

A special note should be made of what is today the most controversial weapon of the ninja: the shuriken. Also called the throwing star, death star or ninja star, this weapon is included in other martial arts systems. It was originally a straight piece of metal, variously edged and pointed at one or both ends, but over the centuries the ninja and other men of war fashioned it in different ways; sometimes it was star-shaped, with the number of points varying from school to school. Techniques and methods of use also varied; sometimes the

Top row: a bear hug from the rear opens this attack, followed by a backward strike to the face of the attacker and an upward sweep of the arms to break his hold. Even though his grip may be strong initially, the blow to the face weakens it.

Bottom row: the defender shifts his weight to the right, seizes the attacker and throws him forwards onto his back.

shuriken were thrown at the opponent, while at other times they were scattered on the ground for the enemy and their luckless horses to tread on.

Because a few hooligans have used these stars in public, there has been an outcry in the West, demanding that the shuriken should be banned from sale. The fact that the press had also from time to time reported the throwing of darts at football matches, by rival supporters, not to mention broken bottles and other missiles, was conveniently forgotten. From the point of view of accuracy and danger, a dart is much more deadly than any shuriken on sale today.

Training in the use of the shuriken is very difficult and highly structured. The great exponent of the art is Shirakami Ikku-ken, author of *Shuriken-do – My Study of the Way of the Shuriken*, published in 1987. Shirakami became interested in throwing techniques as a boy, and was fortunate enough to be taken on as a pupil by Master Naruse Kanji of the famous Negishi Ryu. From then on he devoted all his spare time to the technique and history of his art, covering not only shuriken techniques but also hatchet throwing, knife throwing, boomerang throwing and baseball pitching. In the end there was virtually nothing that he could not throw with consummate skill.

In his book Shirakami demonstrates the use of the shuriken as an ancillary weapon to the sword. He shows how it may be passed rapidly from one hand to the other and sent spinning towards the enemy. His research also revealed that a type of shuriken was dropped from a great height by the pilots of the tiny aeroplanes used in World War I.

Combining his technical knowledge with a study of Japanese military and religious history, Shirakami evolved an outlook on life intimately linked with the shuriken; for him it has truly become a 'way' or philosophy. A notable success in his life concerned a local schoolboy hooligan who was neglecting his work and earning a bad reputation in the district. This youth asked Shirakami to teach him the shuriken. With some misgivings, mixed with hopes for the boy's redemption, Shirakami agreed. The new pupil showed real skill, and such was his satisfaction at being able to do one thing well that it spilled over into other areas of his life. In time the former hooligan became a graduate and a respectable member of the society which at one time had rejected him.

This story is a long way from the ancient ninja and the Shimabara wars, but it illustrates another side of the martial arts which in our crumbling world we might well remember.

77

SUMO

Above: sumotori (sumo students)
staging a contest in the dohyo, a special
circle in which all bouts take place.
Above right: limbering up with the
special crouching and leg-raising
exercises essential for sumo fighters.

Sumo is the art of giants. The sight of men weighing
up to 215 kilos, moving across the clay ring like
human battering rams, has thrilled Japanese spectators for centuries. Today, in the West, notably in
France, both live and television presentations are
attracting a wide audience. There are no weight
categories in sumo, but sometimes contestants giving away more than 70 kilos have defeated their
heavier opponents. The bouts or basho are staged
with all the panoply of a state occasion; it is after
all 'the sport of emperors'. In the *Nihon Shoki*, a

collection of Japanese legends and old tales, the story is told of how the eleventh emperor of Japan, Suinin, witnessed a battle to the death between an unusually tall champion and a rival. In those days the rules of sumo, originally called sumai, were less stringent and the giant kicked, threw and trampled his opponent to death.

Even with modern rules it is a mistake to equate the art with wrestling. A basho begins with both contestants or sumotori entering the specially built and purified clay ring. Each man tries to 'psych out' his opponent, stamping on the ground, walking about the area and throwing salt around him, to purify the place further, according to Shinto ritual. In the past, this period of preparation could last a long time, but today there is a time limit. In the end, under the supervision of the referee or gyogi, the two men bend forward in the centre of the circle.

As soon as the fists of both men touch the ground, they may begin fighting. In general, they immediately hurl themselves forward. The aim is to throw or drive the other man outside the ring, to throw him to the ground, or to make any part of his body except his feet touch the ground. To perform any of these actions requires considerable skill.

The rules of sumo allow contestants to push, pull, slap or grapple and to seize the mawashi or silk cloth covering the loins and genitals, although only the part which goes around the waist may be used for this purpose. Balance and the keeping and losing of it is a crucial part of sumo technique; sometimes a man may be about to be pushed from the ring when suddenly he turns, delivers a powerful slap to push his opponent off balance and drives him out instead. This technique is called uttchari.

Sumotori usually begin training in their teens

and frequently come from agricultural or fishing backgrounds, where the work has already built up strong loins and legs. The Japan Sumo Association lays down guidelines concerning minimum height and weight, and sees that these are enforced. Beginners spend up to six months in a kind of preparatory school or kyoshujo where they learn all the technical and ritual aspects of the art. They then go on to join one of the sumo stables where they encounter a hierarchical system in which they must serve the senior sumotori; in addition to their training they do all the menial work, cleaning the training areas and even cooking and serving the giant meals consumed by the seniors. It is said that this early culinary experience and their love of food is the reason why so many sumotori open up restaurants when they retire. Once they are deemed sufficiently skilful, the recruits enter the jo-no-kuchi, the lowest division of the ranks. There are four lower ranks to be struggled through before a man can enter the juryo class. In time, if he is good enough, a sumotori may rise to the yokozuna level, becoming a grand champion. During a basho the lower four ranks fight only seven rounds, while the upper ranks fight fifteen. At the end of a basho there are not only awards for winning but also for showing the most skill and exhibiting the most fighting spirit. In addition to their prize money, the sumotori receive financial help from the very active fan clubs, which also provide them with some of their expensive ceremonial garments. They may also be supported by wealthy patrons and by commercial interests looking for popular personalities to publicize their products or services.

It is hard to look at a sumotori without thinking that he is just an extremely fat man. Incredible though it may seem, however, the amount of fat on these mammoth beings is small. There is surface fat but beneath it is strong muscle. One of the few foreign sumotori to win fame in Japan, Konishiki of Hawaii, said that he shed tears at the severity of his training. This shows that the muscle must be there, somewhere.

Hawaii is the chief place outside Japan where sumo is actively pursued. The Hawaiian Sumo Association was founded in the 1920s and holds regular basho. In 1963 Jesse Kuhaulua, whose pro-

Top: tachi-ai, the first and sudden attack of a sumo contest, in which the contestants hurl themselves forward like human battering rams. This first attack can signal the downfall of either man if his opponent can make him fall forwards.
Centre: yori-taoshi, a rapid and powerful throw to the ground.
Bottom: shitate-nage, one of the 48 recognized sumo techniques or shijuhatte, involving a strong sideways push.

fessional sumo name became Takamiyama – high view mountain – was spotted on the island. He went to Japan, became a member of the Takasago stable, and in 1967 was the first non-Japanese to reach the juryo class. By 1972 he had crowned that achievement by winning a championship and being awarded the Emperor's Cup. Far from being disliked by the Japanese sumo fans as one might have feared, he was taken to their hearts. Twelve years later another Hawaiian, known in Japan as Konishiki, rocked the sumo world by defeating two grand champions only two years after taking up the sport. It is difficult to imagine what the Western equivalent of such an achievement could be, but perhaps it is like someone taking up boxing and after two years winning the heavyweight championship of the world. Takamiyama discovered Konishiki, who was born of Samoan parents; in 1988 he is still among the best of the sumotori.

One might be forgiven for thinking that sumotori are nothing but huge fighting machines, but Konishiki was originally destined to become a lawyer, and his mental ability has been invaluable during his meteoric rise. He became proficient in the Japanese language within two years, and constantly strives to analyse and perfect his fighting techniques. All the sumo stable masters were astounded at his speed of learning. His other skills include playing the trombone and trumpet.

To appreciate sumo more fully one needs to understand something of the national religion of Shinto. This peculiarly Japanese faith is pantheist. Behind the visible and living world exists a world of kami. The meaning of kami cannot be directly translated into another language, but a word such as 'spirits' might suffice. There are kami in everything, and there are the kami of dead ancestors. Shinto doctrine states that the kami are coexistent with life on earth; they influence it and are influenced by it. When doing anything, a human being should take the kami into account. They may be displeased and make their displeasure felt in quite tangible ways. To show respect to the kami, the Shinto faith has many ceremonies which are instrumental in maintaining good relations with them. Sumo contests themselves were at one time seen in a ceremonial light, being a kind of offering to the kami, and this is why the existing rituals of the art

Top: *yorikiri, a favourite throwing hold in which the belt is gripped and the opponent lifted, turned and deposited on the ground.*
Centre: *the palms of the hands shoot forward, searching for a grip on the belt or a push, known as tsuki.*
Bottom: *uwate-dashi-nage, a throw using pressure on the arms.*

are so carefully maintained and observed. To fail to do this would bring bad results for those who were guilty of omission. In Japan the simultaneous belief in such things and the living of a modern, technologically advanced life are not seen as contradictory. Just as many Christians and Jews believe that the Book of Genesis is true, many Japanese believe that the progenitor of their race was a god, Takemikazuchi, who defeated a commoner in a wrestling match. Somewhere in every sumotori's mind is the knowledge that he is participating in something which lies at the very foundation of his country's existence. Another example of sumo's place in the beliefs of the Japanese is what is called 'sumo in the mud'. Annually, the young men in the farming villages fight in thick mud; the muddier they become the better the harvest will be.

Surprisingly, there are few serious injuries in sumo. This is due to the superb fitness of the participants. During the 1920s a sumotori called Dewa-ga-Take, who weighed around 180 kilos, accidentally killed his opponent in the ring. After that encounter he was forbidden to use various sumo techniques. This single tragedy, compared with the fatalities which have occurred in other sports, only emphasizes its safe nature. Safety is further assisted by the divisions referred to earlier, which keep the less skilful sumotori out of reach of the more accomplished men. Complete mismatches, such as one often sees in Western boxing, are virtually unknown. One contestant may beat another quickly, but all sumo contests are quick, so the speed of victory is not an indication of a 'walkover' triumph. Once he is a recognized professional, a sumotori fights at 15 basho every year, and also takes part in exhibition and promotional bouts. This imposes quite a strain on his energy reserves, so he must know how to pace himself through the season. Unlike a Western boxer or wrestler, a sumotori cannot maintain his position unless he fights in all the scheduled bouts. If he is laid off consistently, even on account of injury, he slips down the ranks and others replace him. Few fighters carry on beyond the age of 30, and those who have reached the higher divisions are by that time quite wealthy. A popular champion continues to be held in high esteem after he has retired; as well as opening a business, he may continue to maintain an interest in the art by coaching youngsters and by scouting for new talent. On retirement, a sumotori attends a special ceremony at which other fighters cut off his topknot of hair or chonmage, as a sign that he is no longer one of them.

In recent years foreigners or gaijin from many countries have taken up sumo in Japan, and the art is slowly spreading across the West.

Opposite page: *uwate-nage, known as a 'simple throw'. The literal meaning of the expression is 'better hand throw'.*

Above: *tsuri-dashi, a throwing technique in which the belt is seized with a sudden snatching movement.*

Below: *nodowa-zeme, a quick push to the throat, produces a loss of balance or distracts attention momentarily.*

Above: the formal salute of Shorinji Kempo with the hands held in front of the face, the fingers widespread.
Below: one of the powerful punches of the art, shown from three angles. Note the bent rear leg and slightly inclined trunk.

Opposite page: when Shorinji Kempo students sit in a meditation posture the staff is sometimes used to correct the position of the back.

SHORINJI KEMPO

Shorinji Kempo is registered in Japan as a religion and not as a martial art. It was conceived before World War II when the late grandmaster of the system, Doshin So, spent some time in China as a secret agent and also studied a number of Chinese fighting methods. Although these methods would be popularly known as kung fu today, in China they are also referred to as 'ch'uan fa', meaning 'fist way', or simply 'boxing'. The Japanese word for ch'uan fa is kenpo or kempo. Shorinji is Japanese for Shaolin-ssu, so the name means Shaolin Temple boxing.

Doshin So brought back to Japan the knowledge and methods he had learned in China and founded a school of his own. Although originally Shorinji Kempo was started as a secret organization, the grandmaster later opened his doors to avoid 'the danger of degeneration or of a transmission of mistaken ideas about Shorinji Kempo'. Today the Shorinji Kempo organization is worldwide and has the distinction of containing both a lay and a religious division. The latter follows the Kongo Zen school and its members are distinguished by their shaven heads.

In 1970 Doshin So wrote a large tome about his style which was welcomed by the martial arts world. He saw his art as a way of life, 'based on the realization of the interrelation and interaction of all things and knowledge, and Man's potentialities as the only tools with which he can successfully traverse life'. The ultimate objective of the art is 'to alleviate suffering and secure happiness on earth'. To this end the philosophy of Shorinji Kempo seeks to combine the material benefits of the West and the spiritual and moral discipline of the East. One of the avowed aims of Shorinji Kempo teaching is to make its students care about other people, 'living half for oneself and half for others'.

Undoubtedly, Shorinji Kempo is a fascinating and complete system deserving respect and attention. The latest reports in September 1988 indicate that changes have taken place since its inception in Japan, but as these are relatively minor the techniques and ideas laid down by the founder will be considered here. In keeping with his own idea of a marriage between East and West, Doshin So sought explanations of the effectiveness of techniques from both sources. Citing the simpler aspects of Western mechanics, he pointed to levers, centrifugal force and the understanding of the principle of the spring to give a grounding for his Kempo methods: '. . . if the arm is used as a spring, strength can be magnified without extra force.' He also brought into focus the Eastern knowledge of vital points on the human body, and the ability to cause pain, paralysis or unconsciousness by using these points. The application of such knowledge is not easy, as is sometimes claimed. Even so, the stress put on such techniques in Shorinji Kempo emphasizes the fundamental thinking of the art: to restrain rather than hurt one's opponent; to hurt him rather than kill him.

Good manners and etiquette are important as one might expect. The traditional Kempo salute involves placing both hands together, with fingers spread out, on a level with the face. This signifies not only respect for the other person but also that 'above Man, there is no man', meaning that all men are equal. Even though all Shorinji Kempo practitioners are individuals, they are not separate but a brotherhood. Cleanliness and tidyness are important, while careless speech and any behaviour which denotes inattention or lack of respect is frowned upon. To assist in the cultivation of the required qualities, a daily session of Zen meditation is part of the Kempo regime. When trying to gain a suitable posture in meditation, students may be helped by a partner who applies a staff to the back to aid an upright posture and may massage the shoulder and neck muscles to free them of tension. This assistance is called seiho. Doshin So's writings and his emphasis on religious themes mark him out as a visionary who saw his system as one of vital importance to the future of mankind. Time will judge whether his vision was accurate.

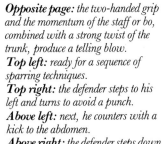

Opposite page: the two-handed grip and the momentum of the staff or *bo*, combined with a strong twist of the trunk, produce a telling blow.
Top left: ready for a sequence of sparring techniques.
Top right: the defender steps to his left and turns to avoid a punch.
Above left: next, he counters with a kick to the abdomen.
Above right: the defender steps down and takes hold with a wrist lock.
Right: he begins to apply the wrist lock, turning his partner to the left.
Below: the attacker begins a breakfall to relieve the pressure on his wrist.
Below right: the defender has still got control of his partner on the ground.

Top: in a 'ready' stance, preparing for a sparring sequence.
Second from top: the man on the right tries a face punch which is blocked.
Second from bottom: the defender follows his block with a wrist lock.
Bottom: the attacker must breakfall to save his wrist.
Opposite page, top left: a man armed with a staff prepares to attack an unarmed partner.
Top centre: as the attack develops, the defender withdraws his weight onto his back leg and leans away.
Top right: as the attack comes in, the defender leans even further away to avoid it.
Second row, left: the defender ducks under the staff, moving to the opposite side of it.
Second row, centre: he rapidly moves in, preparing to launch a kick.
Second row, right: the kick strikes the target.
Below right: a typical Shorinji Kempo wrist lock, applied after throwing a partner. The hold on the wrist is reinforced with control from the leg.

In the traditional vein Shorinji Kempo stresses the importance of correct stances. It uses a terminology which differs from the mainstream of karate expressions and as such points up the difficulty of correctly describing a stance using only a few words. The stance 'chudan gamae' or 'chudan kamae' means 'middle level stance'; this involves standing with one leg forward, the other back and both hands held between the shoulders and waist, the middle level of Japanese martial arts. The choice of words indicates the part of the stance which is being emphasized, i.e. the protection of the middle region. The same stance, with the left hand open instead of closed in a fist, is called 'ichiji gamae' or 'flat-hand stance', emphasizing the one open palm and not the middle region. In most of the popular Japanese karate systems the word used to describe a stance is 'dachi' and not 'gamae', which in karate is used to indicate the idea of 'guard' rather than 'stance'. 'Fukko gamae' or kneeling stance is rarely found in other martial arts, except as a passing movement of pentjak silat (see page 156), and is one of the remarkable features of Shorinji Kempo.

Because the art relies heavily on evasive tactics, footwork is important in training. Shorinji Kempo students must be light and quick on their feet and this is facilitated by training in the cross-over step, the side step and the step dodge, as well as other methods of moving out of the line of fire. Part of this training includes the use of breakfalls to avoid attack, a technique also used in ninjutsu (see page 70). In Shorinji Kempo breakfalls also include cartwheels.

'Blocking techniques are the most basic' was

one of Doshin So's tenets, and the mechanics of blocking an attack using the hands and arms are explored by students. The techniques are divided into those which apply force at right angles to an arm or leg, those which use a curving action, and those which attempt to apply a minimum of force, taking advantage of the attacker's own force to achieve the objective. The upward block or uwa-uke is reminiscent of the palm change used in pakua (see page 126). Thrusting or punching methods are the same or similar to those used in karate and kung fu, with more stress on turning and 'leaning into' a technique than one finds in traditional karate. Kicking techniques are also similar to those used in karate. When training in two-man sparring begins the differences between Shorinji Kempo and karate or any current kung fu form become clearer. Traditional karate uses a fairly upright stance, and many kung fu styles have characteristic, classic stances which immediately identify them. In the Kempo two-man sparring forms it is evident that a kind of rolling of the hips is combined with leaning movements of the trunk to provide continuous, circular action. This, combined with the evasive stepping techniques, gives the art its distinctive quality.

The use of locking techniques or techniques for evading a lock or grip are given as much atten-

tion as they are in aikido or jujutsu and the similarities are inescapable. Once the various intricacies of wristwork are understood, students can combine this knowledge with supplementary methods from other areas of the art; for example, a wrist lock escape can be followed up with a punch.

Although Shorinji Kempo has unique characteristics, it may safely be said that the throwing techniques of the art can be found by combining judo, aikido and jujutsu methods. A noteworthy method of taking falls is to land on the soles of the feet before letting the back meet the ground. Once an opponent is down, there are various methods of keeping him there, mainly using locks on the shoulder, elbow and wrist.

The standard clothing for training sessions in Shorinji Kempo is similar to a karate uniform, but many martial artists retain the image of the Kempo student in his distinctive ceremonial monk's robe, which symbolizes the art's religious basis. The robe is held in place by a thick, cotton-filled, tubular belt.

Today, Shorinji Kempo is held in high esteem in the martial arts world, but as most people do not want to be involved in Zen meditation or have no wish to relate their martial arts to an oriental religious belief, it is unlikely that it will ever become as widespread as karate or judo, which are not committed in that direction. However, those interested in taking up the art will have no difficulty in finding a teacher. Physically, Shorinji Kempo is as demanding as any combination of karate, judo and aikido might be. The student must not only kick and punch, but also throw and be thrown. To use a phrase which has found its way into the vernacular, it is a 'total martial art'.

Top left: ready to begin a sparring sequence, with the leading hand in a blocking position and the rear hand ready to punch.
Top right: the man on the left begins a kicking attack and his partner withdraws onto one leg.
Above: as the kick arrives, the defender has his arms raised to protect his face or the side of his body.
Opposite page, above left: this sequence begins with the man on the right anticipating his partner's attack.
Opposite page, above right: as the attacker moves in, the defender turns him.
Opposite page, below left: the defender continues to turn his partner, beginning a throw.
Opposite page, below right: the throw is completed.

JODO

The story of jodo – the way of the short stick or staff – illustrates a recurring theme in the history and legend of martial arts. It is that of supernatural revelation of a particular style or technique. Modern psychologists might explain such phenomena in terms of subconscious desires or the result of stress, but as most martial arts originated in countries with a shamanist or pantheistic culture, where every object and living thing has its own characteristic spirit, the idea of a godlike inspiration as a source of innovation is more fitting.

Such a revelation was experienced by Muso Gonnosuke at the turn of the sixteenth century. This Japanese samurai had taken a not uncommon step. He had decided to wander through the country, testing his skill with the bo, a 2-metre oak staff. Time and again he defeated other weapons masters. News of his exploits reached the ears of an even more famous fighter, Miyamoto Musashi, the Sword Saint as he is sometimes called. Musashi was also undefeated. His technique was so powerful that he had killed using only a wooden sword, and he decided to take up the challenge of the bo master. At the appointed time the two men met, and Musashi, parrying Muso's attack, could have despatched him to the other world. Uncharacteristically, the swordsman spared his life. Despairing and downcast, the defeated man continued to roam and study, racked by the memory of his only failure.

One night, when Muso was fast asleep, an angelic youth appeared to him in a dream, told him that he should devise a new, shorter weapon, and explained how it should be used. Muso awoke and

Opposite page: training with the jo and boken (wooden sword), the man on the right with the jo makes contact with his opponent's weapon.

Above left: by driving the blade of the boken down, he is able to thrust to the face or neck.
Above right: the man on the right blocks a descending sword cut before it reaches him.

began perfecting 12 techniques with a 'jo', a new weapon just like the one he had been shown in his dream. He called this new system jojutsu, as it was then purely a combat system. Seeking out Musashi, he challenged him to a second contest. This time, Musashi was the one whose life was spared.

After his victory, Muso gave his name to the Shindo Muso Ryu, a school which put special emphasis on the jo. For centuries jo techniques were studied by generation after generation of martial men and women. The founder of judo, Jigoro Kano, was pleased to accept the jo into the judo syllabus as a defensive weapon. Then, during the 1950s, a 'do' form of the art was derived from the many 'jutsu' forms, and the All-Japan Jodo Renmei (Federation) was formed. Later, the All-Japan Kendo Renmei took a limited number of techniques and created a syllabus which is now studied by many kendo enthusiasts. It should be made clear that this new syllabus, which is likely to become the most widespread in the West, is but a small part of the original jutsu form. It is to be hoped that this will not cause the older forms to be lost.

The jo is a staff about 125 centimetres long, and 2½ centimetres thick. The best jo are made of white oak, the water content making them quite heavy. A jo made by traditional methods and not mass produced is quite expensive, but if properly used and cared for, it will last a long time. In spite of the fact that it is not a sword, and does not carry the mystery and spiritual qualities of the steel weapon in

the Japanese mind, the jo should not be underestimated. It is a weapon of great power and can snap a sword or smash a sword from the holder's grip. Like the bo, either end can be used, and the special grips which bring about the reversal of the weapon build up tremendous speed and force. In some people's opinion, the jo is much more dangerous than the sword when used correctly. Its use carries with it all the ceremony associated with iaido (see page 48); the clothing worn is similar, and the physical demands are at least as great.

Very few dojo teach only the jo. It is most likely to be found in training halls where kendo, iaido or other Japanese weapons systems are taught, as part of a larger syllabus. This may be because no sporting or competitive form has been developed for it. Strikes with the jo are too powerful for the type of armour worn in kendo, and armour which would withstand such strikes would be so thick that the movements of the participants would be impeded. It remains for some enterprising sports equipment manufacturer using modern ballistic materials to come up with a solution.

Despite its relative obscurity, the jo is an interesting weapon to study. Its length, being almost comparable with the sword, produces some techniques and on-guard positions reminiscent of those used in kendo and iaido. As in several other Japanese martial arts, the human body is divided into three sections for purposes of defining target areas. These are the jodan or upper level, the chu-

Above: with strong pressure on the jo, he forces his opponent's arms up and back.

Above: the leverage and power of a jo attack is clearly demonstrated as the man on the right moves forward.
Below: the man armed with the boken is forced to give ground.

dan or middle level, and the gedan or lower level. Strikes with the jo are divided into these three areas, as are the defensive movements and on-guard positions. Attacks with the jo can be described as swings or sweeps, and thrusts. The latter are hard to stop as they are difficult to see. Either end of the jo can be used to attack or defend, and the methods of changing one's grip to facilitate this are taught to the beginner.

As in the iaido or kendo dojo, students are shown how to stand in a formal fashion and must not wander about or fiddle with their staffs. The required posture, called ritsu jo, is a kind of simple standing to attention with the jo resting on the floor vertically, held by the left hand. A different holding position, using the right hand, is used for carrying the jo about. Apart from the basic grips and stances, beginners are also taught methods of stepping.

Although jodo can be performed solo, in the syllabus adopted by the kendo fraternity it is used against a wooden sword or boken, and in demonstrations it is usually the more senior of the two contestants who holds the sword. Training in the two-man forms consists of a series of short exchanges in which the person holding the jo finally defeats his partner by a series of defensive and offensive movements. This formal training is not as rigid as it may seem; many a slip can occur and both men need to be alert and watchful, especially where timing, and halting a technique before the jo strikes one's partner, is concerned. As no armour is worn, a certain degree of courage is needed to train freely with the jo, and a definite trust in one's partner. Each needs to feel confident that the other will not get carried away and deliver an actual blow.

The techniques used by the kendo fraternity in jo training are limited. Entwining techniques, the study of attacking vital spots or atemi, and much more of the jojutsu repertoire are missing. The versatile jo was welcomed not only by Jigoro Kano of judo fame, but also by the founder of aikido (see page 24), Morihei Uyeshiba. The parts of the jodo system that have been absorbed into the aikido syllabus are called aiki-jo and are aimed at displaying aikido movements, utilizing the jo, rather than simply teaching the straightforward and much more aggressive jojutsu techniques. Because of this the movements of aiki-jo are often found to be slower and less combat-oriented than those used in jodo.

Aiki-jo techniques include methods of taking the jo from an attacker and keeping the jo in one's hand during such an attempt. There are also throwing techniques where the defender uses the opponent's hold on the jo to throw him, staff and all. Aiki-jo features methods of fighting with jo against jo, making for a much more stimulating exchange of blows than when the boken is used against the jo. The profound influence of body movement peculiar to aikido appears in its use of the staff and this also contributes to the differences in approach of the two styles. This is inevitable, as someone who is fundamentally an aikido man cannot change his spots and become a sword or jo master too, unless he is truly exceptional. Aikido has a softer, more harmonious approach. However, the use of the jo is explored in the full aikido syllabus without detracting from its use as a dangerous weapon.

For a full exploration of the jo in its 'jutsu' as well as its 'do' forms, students should have satisfactory circulatory and respiratory systems combined with adequate joint function. To be able to advance, retreat, sink and rise swiftly in a supple manner qualifies anyone for jodo training. Age is no barrier; indeed, youthful energy can blind its possessor to what he is doing, leading him to exaggerate his movements, which stifles the continuity of his effort and makes him vulnerable. A turn of the wrist at the right moment can change defeat into victory. So too much strength, too much energy, should be tempered by a search for technical exactness.

KIAI

The use of sound in war and peace has played an important part in human life. In war, the skirl of the bagpipes has stirred the blood of many a Scottish regiment far from home, while the rhythms played on the war drums of the North American Indians prior to battle helped to induce a fearless state of mind. There are many other examples. Similarly, the use of chanting and singing to stir the spirits of cold or frightened men and women has been found throughout the history of all nations; it has also been used to express their joy at being alive and well. The final scene of Kurosawa's film *The Seven Samurai* contrasts so vividly with all the preceding scenes because of its sound content: the peasants, freed for a time from the threat of death and oppression, sing together as they plant the new rice crop.

In the martial arts world one particular sound, which features prominently in Japanese systems, is the kiai. This is sometimes translated as 'union of spirit', but as is generally the case with little-understood matters, the debate over the meaning of the word rages interminably.

In practice the kiai takes the form of a shout emitted at the moment of an attack, or sometimes prior to it. Although it is most commonly associated with swordplay, it is also present in other martial arts. The explanation of the purpose of this shout is that it unnerves, paralyses or hypnotizes one's adversary, or at least makes him pause, and in the same split second he can be cut down. In the animal world, the growl of an adult tiger or the roar of a lion instils fear into most creatures and may paralyse some. In everyday life a sudden shout, uttered unexpectedly, can freeze a person standing near. These are instances in which no special preparation has been made by the animal or human producing the sound. But in the case of Japanese warriors, as with anything the Japanese undertake, the investigation into the use of the kiai was thorough and persistent.

Assistance in this study was often sought from Zen Buddhist masters, whose knowledge of the inner life of man, and acquaintance with the role of the lower abdomen or hara in meditation, was renowned. There is no doubt that the centring of one's energy in the lower abdomen enables one to release it suddenly in the form of sound, with a devastating effect. The author has personal experience of one case where a man was suddenly and unexpectedly subject to such a shout; it made him almost literally jump out of his skin and he experienced adverse effects for days afterwards. Stories are told of martial arts masters who could kill with the kiai. Others are known to have used its unexpressed power to walk through packs of marauding wolves, and this underlines the idea that the kiai as a shout is only one example of the working of an unknown inner power. The old adage that one should look a wild beast in the eye to subdue him indicates a common belief in such things.

The utterance of the kiai in martial arts does not seem to depend on any particular vowel sound or consonant. Sometimes it is brief; sometimes it is long and varying in pitch, even beautiful. When one hears a long kiai uttered by someone knowledgeable in its production, one can sense the sudden release and fading of a definite inner quality, like a gigantic wave which crashes upon the shore, only to be recalled into the limitless ocean, hissing among shingle and sand. One should not forget of course that sound in human beings is intimately related to breath, and breathing features prominently in Zen meditation training, where it is seen as closely connected with thought control, and the subsidence of thoughts of a distracting nature.

These few paragraphs are intended to give a brief outline of a subtle and profound subject.

CHINESE KUNG FU

The Chinese lion, the huge drum and
the strong stance of the drummer
combine to give an impression of
beauty, strength and bright colour.
These ingredients, plus an astonishing
agility, are all part of the performance
which is to follow.

Was that a dragon which glittered through the mist? Was that a monkey, cavorting and skittering through the dust – or a man? Did a tiger suddenly strike from the pale bamboo or a human arm streak into view? Such questioning images readily fill one's mind when faced with the endless panorama of Chinese kung fu.

Kung fu is more than a martial art. The Chinese regard it as part of the historical tapestry of their lives. Like blue merging into violet, it does not begin here and end there. It is simultaneously legend, history, medicine, combat, dance, theatre and physical culture. Therein lies much of the misunderstanding that arose in the West when kung fu suddenly blossomed in a myriad forms in the 1970s. New kung fu magazines desperately tried to fill the knowledge gap. The kung fu television series starring David Carradine, followed by the Japanese dramatization of the Chinese epic *The Water Margin* and many lesser film presentations, informed the martial-arts hungry public. But how could anyone pack three thousand years of culture into a few hours of viewing time?

Plainly it was impossible. Kung fu is one example of the long-standing attempt by the West to find a response to the civilizations of the East. We know that there is something there which we want, but what is it? Do the spirits of kung fu masters, their secrets safe, mock us from a Taoist heaven, or do they smile with approval at our efforts to understand them for ourselves? The West is indeed struggling manfully to do this. Time and again Western students make the pilgrimage to Eastern countries to increase their knowledge. They bring back more techniques, more sayings, partial insights and souvenirs. Yet all admit, 'It is different in China, in Japan, in Korea . . .' There is it seems something in the air itself, which will not travel; and the nearer one gets to home the more it evaporates.

One of the insights we can intellectually comprehend and much less easily sense and feel is the important idea that everything in the universe consists of the same basic elements and forces, mingling and separating to produce forms of varying duration and with differing qualities. Thus we know that the Chinese have a cycle of years allotted to a series of animals such as the tiger, the dragon, the rat and so on, and that everybody is said to possess some of the characteristics of the animal whose year they are born in. For example, someone born in the year of the rat will be persistent, 'gnawing away' at things until he succeeds.

Just as the mingling and separating of the forces of the universe and nature produces different people in different years, it also produces the wide variety of animal life. The connection continues with kung fu, which has many styles that take the name of a particular animal, as in hsing-i (see page 122). A description of various animal styles can be found on the following pages. One of the most interesting, monkey style kung fu, has the elements of 'monkey-ness' within it. It is quick, unexpected, funny and agile, as well as effective as a combat art. Similarly, praying mantis style has the lightning action of the insect as it seizes its victim. It also has peculiar hand movements, supposed to imitate the grasping action of the mantis.

Other kung fu styles have been revealed in dreams, in visions, in moments of crisis; produced by arduous years of solitary study or in service of an esteemed master; brought from another country and then modified; or adapted from the use of a weapon whose techniques could be seen to work using only the bare hands.

Religious influences appear frequently in the history of kung fu, but going back even further the records of the Shang dynasty, which lasted from the eighteenth to the twelfth century BC, tell of a folk martial art in which people wore animal horns and fought one another, then wrestled to the ground. In the Chou dynasty, circa 1126–255 BC, archery and charioteering were an essential part of the education of all gentlemen and scholars. Also during this dynasty, Confucius was born in China in 551, and the Taoist Lao-tse was alive, his birth date unknown but his death put at 514; the prophet Zarathustra was born in Media in 660, the Buddha was born in India in 563, and Socrates was born in Greece in 489. These significant figures profoundly influenced the current thinking in their respective countries, and their influence spread far and wide.

During the second half of the Chou dynasty, influenced by the Confucian ideas of conduct, a loosely-knit body of men appeared on the scene known as the Chinese knights-errant. These warriors, skilled in martial arts and driven in the main by high ideals, put wrongs to right for rich and poor alike. Centuries later, the influence of the Buddha, in the form of Zen, informed many of the samurai of Japan about how to conduct themselves inwardly, in daily life as well as in battle, and the indefinable spirit of Lao-tse was infused into various Chinese martial arts such as t'ai chi and pakua (see pages 116 and 126). One sees that the religious heirs of these great teachers found ways of elevating martial arts, checking their indiscriminate use, if only a little, and contributing through them to the life of mankind. The martial element mingled with the religious element to produce many new phenomena which were on occasion neither mere fighting nor mere religious observance.

The most important religious influence on Chinese martial arts was Bodhidharma (AD 448–527), who left his Indian retreat to spread the word of the Buddha in China. The approach he taught was known in India as 'dhyana', and in Chinese it was called 'ch'an'. Ch'an Buddhism put emphasis on meditation. After enduring incredible hardships and a less than auspicious interview with the Chinese emperor, Bodhidharma went to the Shaolin Temple in Honan province. Refused entry, he withdrew to a cave where he 'faced the wall' – sat in meditation – for nine years. The story that he cut off his own eyelids to prevent himself from falling asleep during meditation is probably untrue; it may have been invented by overzealous followers, or was used simply to demonstrate an old saying, such as the biblical 'If thine eye offends thee, pluck it out'. An even more unlikely story adds to the drama: the teacher's prolonged gaze is said to have bored a hole in the mountainside, convincing the head of the Shaolin Temple that he should be admitted. What is certain is that Bodhidharma was received there and became the First Patriarch of Ch'an. His iron self-discipline and strength contrasted with that of his new Chinese charges, mainly scribes who had worked for years copying books and doing little prolonged meditation. He compelled them to improve their physical condition by devising a series of exercises, some of them akin to present-day martial arts exercises. One of these, the horse-riding stance in its wide form, appears in many kung fu styles. This period marks the beginning of much of the traditional kung fu (see Wing Chun, page 140). It may also explain the persistent appearance and development of all kinds of calisthenics in China, both as a 'warm up' for martial arts and as a separate discipline.

Most of the subsequent Shaolin styles of kung fu belonged to the hard or external group of styles; it was the Taoist influence which seems to have introduced the softer, internal styles. The expression 'Wu-wei' or 'No action' is linked with the words of Lao-tse. In government, in personal relationships, in every walk of life, the sage or man of Tao does nothing. This idea is beyond explanation in a sense, but one might say that it means that in doing anything the desire to succeed should be absent, as this stands in the way of what one is doing. One should let what one is doing take place, without becoming involved. This approach belongs to arts such as t'ai chi (see page 116) rather than, for instance, the tiger style of kung fu.

The Confucian codes of conduct deeply influenced Chinese life, and respect for authority, for

A high leap in the colourful costume of monkey style kung fu.

one's elders, for the group or family is indelibly stamped on the Chinese character. In the kung fu world, respect for the master is a strong feature and this includes respect for the techniques of the style he teaches. As a result, a style often becomes crystallized, since new ideas are not absorbed, and this can lead to the formation of splinter styles consisting of old and new techniques.

In the past, many kung fu men and women became guards on caravans, instructors in military academies, the personal champions of dignitaries and so on. Today, numerous kung fu men have taken up employment as bodyguards, 'bouncers', or security guards. Some of the best have managed to find fame on the cinema screen, often having begun work as stunt men. A point of interest for fans of kung fu movies is that one of the techniques used to bring off those high leaps is to place springboards at strategic points on a set where dramatic fight scenes are to take place.

The following styles have been chosen because they illustrate the variety of kung fu movements.

Monkey style

In the first quarter of the seventh century AD, an historic journey from China to India was under-

taken by a Buddhist monk, Hsuan Tsang, whose intention was to find the Tripitaka, the Buddhist scriptures. The search lasted for about 16 years, and during this time the monk had as a bodyguard no less a figure than the monkey king himself, Sun Wu-k'ung, known simply as Monkey. 'The nature of Monkey is irrepressible' and this quality, combined with amazing kung fu skills and an incredible dexterity with the monkey cudgel or staff, saved Hsuan Tsang from death scores of times. This folk tale is immortalized in the Chinese classic *Hsi Yo Chi* or *Journey to the West*. In China, Monkey is still regarded by some as a deity and worshipped, although his own attitude to life was less than reverent.

Some of Monkey's characteristics must surely be found in the Ta Sheng style of monkey boxing, which had an interesting beginning. In 1911 a well-known martial artist, Kou Sze, killed a man and was imprisoned for eight years. Near the window of his cell was a thicket in which many monkeys played and fought. Kou Sze became interested in them and began to imitate their way of fighting. Then he combined his newly discovered methods with the martial style he already knew and produced the Ta Sheng style. Although this is not the oldest style of monkey boxing, it is the best-known today.

Within Ta Sheng there are five subdivisions based on observation of the animals themselves. Lost Monkey form was inspired by the monkey in any group who invariably wanders away from the pack and suddenly realizes that he is lost. Recreating this situation, you try to imagine the monkey's

feeling of isolation. Then an enemy appears and you simulate fear, but behind the apparently panic-stricken postures and movements lies a strategy for defeating the misled foe. When performing Lost Monkey, students must combine a cool mind with a 'desperate' body.

The Drunken Monkey form evokes the sight of an animal suddenly intoxicated and out of control. Monkeys were known to eat and drink indiscriminately from market stalls, some of which displayed jars of Chinese wine. The student appears to stumble and lose his balance, and staggers or rolls from side to side. As in Lost Monkey, he is a master of subterfuge, relaxed and watchful, his performance put on to distract and give a false impression to an attacker. At any point in his display he can launch an attack with far from drunken aim and finish the fight.

Not all the monkeys which Kou Sze observed were playful. Some of them stood still and watched, and they gave their name to the Stone Monkey form, particularly suited to people with strong bodies. Stone Monkey does not roll about and pretend, he meets force with force, trading blow for blow; he is the Rambo of the pack. He can also take full blows to the body, using hard qigong (see wushu, page 132).

Tall people, for whom the rolls and squats of Drunken Monkey and Lost Monkey are not so suitable, can take refuge in the Standing Monkey form based on the movements of those animals possessing particularly long arms. Their long reach, as any boxer knows, gives them a distinct advantage when trying to keep an enemy at bay. Powerful arm

swings are part of the Standing Monkey's fighting repertoire.

The fifth form is Wooden Monkey. It is said to be the most devastating and the most sneaky. Like more than one famous general the Wooden Monkey uses retreat, luring the foe to pursue him, only to attack suddenly when this .is the least expected tactic.

In order to be successful at monkey-style kung fu, a student must be able to think himself into a monkey's body. He must imitate its grimaces and quick glances. The most successful monkey stylists are those who seem to be possessed by the monkey as they perform. The present grandmaster of the style, Chan Chiu Chung, is superb in this respect. He appeared in a film called *The Monkey Fist*, which won universal acclaim in martial arts circles, and several of his students have been champions in major kung fu tournaments in Asia. In addition to its mental aspects and its fighting power, monkey style requires more physical agility than most others. It is not one of the most popular styles, perhaps for this reason, but many of its techniques have been borrowed by other martial arts systems.

White crane style

The white crane style, pak hok, is the only major kung fu system with acknowledged Tibetan connections. It is said to have been brought to China by Taoist priests returning from the Himalayas.

The widely accepted account of its genesis in Tibet relates how a monk was one day interrupted in his meditation by the appearance of an ape, trying to rob a crane's nest. The monk naturally expected that the powerful primate would easily succeed in its intention and that the crane would give ground, having no possibility of defending its eggs. Contrary to this, the crane attacked fiercely. Each time the ape tried to grab it, the crane used its wings and feet to move out of range and then countered with its sharp beak. Its skill and swiftness soon discouraged the ape and the crane returned to its nest. The monk, already skilled in various styles of fighting, incorporated some of the bird's methods into a new style which he named white crane. Another version of its journey to China says that descendants of the monk taught it to the imperial guards of the Chinese emperor.

Just like the original bird when faced by the ape, the style emphasizes evasive tactics, waiting for the right moment before making a counterattack. Once that counterattack has begun, however, the student must continue to attack until he is successful or defeated. There are also many weapons techniques in the system, and a minimum of 15 years' training is said to be necessary to master them all.

The movements of the style are large, contrasting with those of the various monkey forms. There is a certain grandeur about them, remi-

Opposite page: six examples of stances from the white crane style of kung fu. A low crouching stance, a high one-legged stance, a forward stretching stance, a cross-legged stance, a kicking stance and a wide horse-riding stance showing the twin 'beaks' of this powerful form of kung fu.

Above: some of the stances shown on the opposite page are used in this series of defensive movements against a punching attack. The defender on the left draws back to avoid the attack, parries the punch, grabs the attacker's arm and punches in reply.

Below: next, he moves in to sweep the attacker's leg from under him to bring him down.

niscent of the bird itself. For striking with the fists, in various formations, the whole body twists, initiated from the small of the back, and the arms are swung like giant wings. An expected part of the style's arsenal is the hand formation in which the fingers and thumb form a beak to 'peck' at the softer, vital areas of the opponent's body. Defensive actions are also large, using the whole arm or leg, and the kicking techniques are larger than those used in Wing Chun.

White crane kung fu is an exhilarating style with enough to offer a potential student to last a lifetime.

Drunken style kung fu

The Water Margin, a massive Chinese epic, deals with events that are supposed to have taken place during the Sung dynasty (AD 960–1279). A collection of honourable men wrongly accused of treason, and others escaping from the law for a variety of reasons, took refuge in the watery wastes of Liang Shan Po. Here they waged endless war on evildoers and corrupt officials in high places, sometimes enduring torture, always loyal to each other in the face of temptation. One of these heroes was Lu Chi Shen. Having become a monk to avoid arrest, he finally fled to this renowned refuge for fugitives and is regarded as one of the founders of the drunken style. Another hero of Liang Shan Po, Wu Sung, also contributed to the style, having killed a tiger with his bare hands while he was intoxicated. No doubt if he had been sober he would have fled for his life. Such a feat, incidentally, is not without its modern equivalent. The mystic karate man, Gogen Yamaguchi of Japan, killed a Manchurian tiger in his youth. More conventional tiger hunting, using a trident-shaped weapon, was not unknown in China, and is part of the pak mei style of kung fu.

Master Leung Ting of Hong Kong, a researcher into kung fu styles, points out that several systems include what are known as 'drunken' movements, indicating that it is the manner of performance that distinguishes them from the other movements in the style. The most popular form of drunken kung fu is the eight drunken immortals style, which is divided into northern and southern sections. The southern forms require drunken facial expressions and small drunken movements, while those from the north involve much more dramatic indications of the drunken state, such as rolling about, somersaulting and falling. A Taoist monk, Red Brow, created the style when he was living in

In this sequence of drunken style kung fu movements, the performer imitates the actions of an intoxicated man who finishes off the last drop of wine in the bottle and begins to fall over on his back.

Above left and right: *the 'drunken' man is attacked with a punch which he manages to parry.*

Above: *turning 'drunkenly' to his left, he sweeps away the attacker's leg (**above right**) and falls in a state of inebriation (**below**) onto the man's body, knocking all the air out of him.*

the Cave of the Eight Immortals. He adopted a baby boy, but when the time came for him to teach the youth his kung fu style, he was too old to be able to do so. Instead, he wrote instructions in the form of a verse on the wall of the cave, and added some drawings showing how to carry out the movements. After Red Brow's death the boy, Chiu Wan Lung, was unable to get into the spirit of the drawings until one day, a little the worse for drink, he began to try out the movements once more. Suddenly, everything became clear – he had cracked the system.

The actions of the drunken style are relaxed and supple as one might expect. There is much swaying back and forth and from side to side, the arms rising and falling in harmony with the body movement. There are punches and blocking movements and also a number of wrestling-type throws, as well as methods of fighting on and from the floor. Within the main set of movements performed alone, there are some which are reminiscent of the white crane, monkey and other kung fu styles. This underlines the fact that few styles are absolutely pure.

Praying mantis

Master Wong Long founded the praying mantis or tong long system in the seventeenth century. He came from a well-to-do family living in Shantung province, and as a boy he studied martial arts at the Hor Nan Shaolin Temple. He often tried, unsuccessfully, to defeat the senior pupil in his class. Then one day he observed the conflict between a mantis and another insect. After a short while the latter lay dead. With exemplary patience Wong continued to study the martial ways of the victorious mantis. When he believed that he had understood them, he went away and combined them with techniques from many other styles to produce his own praying mantis style. After three years he defeated the senior student. This tale illustrates the traditional patience, one might even say obsession, of the greatest martial arts exponents. It is worth noting that among the styles which have loaned their techniques to the mantis style is the monkey style.

In 1747 Sheng Hsiao, a surgeon, took up the mantle of the mantis and passed on the art to Lee Sam Chin, or Lightning Fist as he was later known. Another disciple of the style, Fan Yook Tung, weighed around 127 kilos and killed two charging bulls using an iron palm technique (see page 113). The Japanese occupation of China drove one of the twentieth-century masters of mantis abroad and the style travelled with him to many places in South and Southeast Asia, where it put down roots. Wong Hon Fan was one of the most famous modern masters of the style and in Europe one of his pupils, Un Ho Bun, keeps the praying mantis flag flying.

Opposite page: *some of the numerous kung fu striking hand positions. These three belong to the praying mantis style.*
Above left: *an example of the powerful swinging movements of kung fu which can be used to block an attack or (**above centre**) to deliver a counterattack to the jaw, for instance.*
Above right: *following up his defence and counter, the man on the right moves in with a grappling technique.*

Below left: *he continues his counterattack.*
Below right: *next, he delivers a punch to his attacker's floating ribs.*

Top left: *both men in a 'ready' stance prior to training.*
Top right: *the man on the left punches, but is blocked by the defender.*

Above left: *the defender then grabs the attacker by the wrist.*
Above right: *he pulls the attacker forwards and chops to the waist.*

Top left: *the man on the left grabs his partner by the wrist.*
Top right: *his partner responds with a blow from his free arm which forces the grip loose.*

Above left: *the defender drives the arm away and keeps contact with it.*
Above right: *the defender slips his blocking arm under and over the attacker's arm, to deliver a punch to the jaw.*

Opposite page, top: *two lion dancers prepare to get into the lion costume.*
Opposite page, below left: *the lion costume is raised high as the dancers take up their positions.*
Opposite page, below right: *the lion dancers are now ready to begin.*

Above: *the lion stands up, ready to face any challengers.*

The most distinguishing feature of the style is the mantis claw, a fist formation in which the index and middle finger are thrust forward, supported by the thumb, and the two other fingers are bent back towards the wrist. This formation imitates the jagged 'teeth' of the insect's claws, with which it seizes its prey. It is used by human practitioners to grab the wrist or elbow of an opponent. Other unusual 'fists' used in mantis are the short and long eagle claws which can dig into the flesh and put pressure on the body's vital spots. One of the notable positions of the style is known as the women's stance: one leg is crossed over the other, to protect the groin area from kicks or other attacks.

The sets of praying mantis movements are demanding, swift and fascinating. Within them one finds punches and kicks, throwing moves, grasping and pulling, and locking of the joints. It takes seven years to become really proficient in the art. There are also two-man sets in which one man attacks with a pre-arranged series of movements and the other defends and counters. Such exercises are absorbing and enable students to learn the mantis techniques without running the risk of being hurt.

Lion dancing

A certain Chinese emperor lay sleeping. In his dreams, danger threatened him, but suddenly a lion came to his rescue and he awoke, safe! Immediately, the emperor sent out a proclamation that in future the lion as a species should be treated with respect and recognized for its brave act. His people were to make images of lions which would be used for special celebrations and festivals, to bring good fortune and dispel evil. Not all lions fared as well as this dream lion. Once, a village was terrorized by a marauding lion. When the villagers managed to catch it, they chopped off its head. In spite of what it had done, it went straight to heaven where the Chinese goddess of mercy, Kwan Yin, took pity on its decapitated condition and using her own red scarf miraculously tied its head back on. She then placed a small mirror on the lion's head, to ward off evil. From then on the lion dance became a feature of Chinese life.

It is difficult to place the dance historically because accounts and dates vary. Some writers say that the lion dance actually came from India, brought by wandering troupes of jugglers and entertainers, during the T'ang dynasty (AD 618–906). The lion is an emblem of the Buddha and the ceremony of Shua Shih Tzu or Exercising the Lions is used to exorcize demons. Lions, like domestic cats, are said to love playing with balls, and during the nineteenth century the yellow and blue lions of the period were often featured in dances

doing just that. The dance was prominent during the festival of the harvest moon.

Thus the lion is sacred to the Chinese and at the beginning of any new enterprise, be it a wedding or the opening of a new office block, a lion dance is required. Whenever you see a lion dance, the red scarf and the mirror of goddess Kwan Yin will be found around his neck and on his head.

It is mainly in kung fu clubs that the study of lion dancing is found today. When a club gets a new lion it must go through a ceremony in which an important person opens the eyes of the lion and dots the eyes, mouth, nose, ears, the back of the head and the mirror. The 'dotting' is carried out to a soft musical accompaniment played on drum, gong and cymbals, but once the lion begins to dance the noise becames deafening. The music follows the tempo of the lion's movements. When he speeds up, so do the musicians. The two men inside the lion do their best to make their movements feline and rhythmic.

There are three types of lion dance. The Beijing lion or Buk-Si is very acrobatic, balancing on a large ball; the performers must be able to 'walk along' on the ball and negotiate a seesaw while making lion-like gestures. This lion is also used in Beijing Opera, and usually wears yellow coverings and 'trousers'. The southern lion of Futsan-Si is the most famous, being very long in the body, highly colourful and exceptionally fierce in his performance. This lion is also something of a vegetarian for he is obliged to pounce on a ceremonial lettuce during his dance, with all the alacrity he would show if it were a juicy steak. Hok Saan-Si is the third type of lion, very popular with the Malaysian Chinese and in Singapore. He is a blend of the first two lions, with a shorter body than the southern lion.

The longer the beard of the lion, the longer the school it represents has been in existence, and when dancing with an older lion, a young lion should show respect. Also, a lion with a black beard is always very fierce and will challenge the lions of other clubs to mock combat. Lion dance competitions take place in all parts of the world where Chinese people live, and they attract a great deal of attention. Each lion must show off its skill and negotiate an obstacle course.

Lion dancing is a demanding art for the two performers. They must have stamina, they must work together, and they must be able to perform the many kung fu movements that are part of the dance. But for the traditionalist it is one of the most satisfying martial arts activities as it embodies such a concentration of China's past.

What is 'kung'?

It is clear that hard work, courage and ingenuity are all necessary for the study of kung fu. The word 'kung' in Chinese means all these things and more: it means a kind of concentration of an unremitting quality which keeps the student's mind on what he is doing and pushes him on when his body has decided it is time to stop. 'Kung' development is mainly associated with the external styles of kung fu, while 'chi' development is associated with the internal styles. Through different uses of words by masters and writers, some confusion has arisen over the meaning of a number of words in the martial arts

vocabulary, but the rough definition given above is a good guide. The description of qigong (chi gung or kung) in the wushu section (see page 132) illustrates this problem. One group of kung fu students separates the chi and the kung, and another group puts them together in the same expression. The latter makes a distinction by putting the words soft and hard in front of qigong. The whole matter is made more difficult by the modern Chinese transliteration which uses a different spelling, i.e. Peking is now Beijing.

Each of the techniques used to develop kung produces a different result. For example, iron palm kung produces hands which can withstand impact when striking hard objects; single finger kung produces a finger which can break wood; and horse stance kung produces a stance which borders on the immovable. Traditionally, there is agreement about what is necessary, from a moral point of view, for the attainment of the best kung. This may be connected with the religious influences on kung fu mentioned earlier. On the one hand there is the training advice, peculiar to each form of kung, and on the other there are things one should not do: one should not be careless, lazy, tense, egoistic, lacking in patience, overindulgent in sex or with alcohol, angry, worried, or overdependent on others. Various specific results are cited if these moral restrictions are not followed. Tension is said to harm the bones, alcohol 'damages' the blood, worry is bad for the brain, anger is detrimental to the heart and lungs, and too much sex weakens all the creative powers. Physical methods of developing kung include massage, repetition of technique, prolonged standing in one position, regulated breathing exercises and weight training. All these external kung practices have as their aim the production of

A technique of thrusting with the long staff, standing on one leg.

a body that can do what most bodies cannot. But these practices only show us what kung can do, not what it is.

Chinese scientists who are investigating the phenomenon claim to have detected some type of invisible wave activity associated with kung which is neither electromagnetic nor infrared, although the production of unusual heat has been observed when kung is manifested. It is possible that there is a perfectly logical explanation. All living organisms have the capacity to protect and heal themselves. As well as the observable activity which accompanies the healing process, there are no doubt other activities which operate at such a fine level that they are not usually observed. If kung training increases the protective process by perhaps 50 or 100 times, then these fine operations may be increased an equal number of times, giving rise to what the Chinese scientists are recording.

Chinese weapons

There are dozens of weapons in the kung fu systems, but each style uses them in its own way. Although their use can be studied in many clubs, the public seem particularly interested in the empty-hand techniques. For some reason the fascination with what an unarmed man can do to defend himself strongly outweighs the interest in his armed potential. It may be because that is how the majority of us see ourselves – without weapons – and we wish

to know what we can do in that condition. Some weapons are illustrated in the Wing Chun and wushu sections of this book.

The chief Chinese martial arts weapons are the double-edged sword, the big knife or broadsword shaped rather like a scimitar, the spear, the halberd, the long and short staffs, various whips, the hammer, the long lance, axes, hooks, knives and the bow and arrow. Among the more exotic weapons is the wolf tooth staff, a long pole with a cluster of metal teeth fixed to a cylinder at one end. It resembles a mace. Another unusual weapon used on horseback was the pen or brush – a long staff which had a carved hand on the end, holding a sharp 'pen' in its grip. Other weapons resembled the harmless cooling fan. Made of bamboo or metal, they were sharpened at the perimeter and sometimes concealed spring-loaded darts.

In the past, the use of weapons in real life by martial men and women depended on many things, such as the type of terrain they lived in, their own build, and the enemy they were facing. Today, the recommended weapons to study are related to range. The usual choice is one weapon for long range – something which can be thrown;

another weapon for medium range, such as a halberd or long staff; a third for close range, such as the double-edged sword; and finally one for very close range, such as a dagger.

Skill in weapons use is regarded by kung fu masters as being on a higher level than empty-hands skill. In particular, skill with the double-edged sword is greatly revered. In legend there are tales of magic swords which bestowed miraculous powers on their owners; others bore a terrible curse.

The Chinese sword is mainly used for thrusting, unlike the samurai sword which is a cutting or slashing blade. As with all weapons, the sword requires dexterity and a good sense of distance. Wrist work is very important, and students are taught how to move the sword in a circle, from the wrist. In the t'ai chi sword schools the index and middle finger of the left hand are held out straight, while the other two fingers are held down by the thumb. The protruding fingers are placed on the pulse of the sword-bearing right arm to give extra 'chi' (see page 117) to it.

An interesting caveat is given to swordsmen: never allow the sword to pass over the fontanel – that part of the top of the skull which closes up last of all during a baby's development – as this is the region that connects the spirit to heaven or the universal intelligence, and to cut through it with the sword would be harmful to the user.

Training with a weapon should not begin until the student has learned a number of empty-hand movements, stances and body shifts. Many of these will be used in weapon play and it is too much of a strain to try to learn everything at once.

Lin kuei – the Chinese 'ninja'

Although much less well known than the Japanese ninja (see page 71), the Chinese lin kuei or forest demons are said to have been the forerunners of the shadow warriors. Their origins are even more obscure than those of the ninja. Some say their martial arts and mystic practices developed from the ways of simple country people, while others claim that they came from Taoists who degraded their religious teaching and used it to mystify, deceive and kill. Whatever the truth may be, the rise in interest in ninjutsu triggered an interest in the lin kuei during the 1980s. Several volumes purporting to be authentic methods of the forest demons appeared on the market, but it is impossible to assess their authenticity. The techniques taught in the name of the lin kuei already exist in orthodox Chinese and Japanese martial arts, and the mystic powers supposedly derived from the study of lin kuei formulae can be found in many books dealing with shamanism and shamanist rites, and also in the thousands of books which Westerners at one time called mumbo jumbo.

Stories also circulated connecting the modern lin kuei with the secret services of various Eastern European countries. There are vestiges of truth in this suggestion, but such is the sophistication of modern espionage techniques, both in the field and in the realm of technology, that the methods of the lin kuei which are of practical use to such organizations must be infinitesimal. The techniques that one imagines would be of use include the ability to become 'invisible', to track an enemy over rough terrain or through forests, to simulate the cries of wild beasts, to hypnotize, to use signs or codes, to escape from bonds by dislocating particular joints, to understand and use poisons, to live off the land, and generally to use in a more primitive way all the skills of a twentieth-century secret agent.

In fairness to the modern lin kuei enthusiasts, the one thing which makes them worthy of serious attention is the care they exercise over detail. Where most people would look at a piece of open ground and see merely grass or bare earth, the lin kuei of ancient times would see a faint imprint of a foot, a speck of spittle or some other indication of the passage of an enemy, and from this would be able to read what the untrained man or woman could not. A foot impression can indicate whether a man is tired, whether he is hurt, whether he is carrying a load, and so on. This is not a matter of supernormal knowledge; it is knowledge which an ordinary person does not think it necessary to possess, or which his powers of observation are not strong enough to give him. The same is true of the resourcefulness of the lin kuei. An ordinary man sees the coins in his pocket as money, the handkerchief for wiping his nose, and his shoe for protecting his foot. The lin kuei can see other uses for these things. The coins can be thrown in an enemy's face, the handkerchief flicked into an enemy's eyes and the shoe filled by his hand to protect his body from a knife.

Like the modern opportunist, the lin kuei saw the world both for what it was and for what it could be in relation to their own aims. Everything had an ulterior use, and this duality was intimately related to the calling of the forest demons.

The theme of duality is relevant to all students of kung fu. When a Western boxer pulls on his gloves and slips his gumshield into place, he purely and simply sees his opponent. When a kung fu student steps into the kwoon he is surrounded by an invisible aura of three thousand years of culture. The Western boxer's aim is to knock his opponent out for the count. The aim of the kung fu student is to celebrate the present and the past.

Above left: *the starting position for basic push hands.*
Above centre: *as the man pushes the woman yields, shifting her weight back.*
Above right: *changing her hand position, the woman pushes the man who in turn yields.*

Below left: *the cycle of pushing begins again as the man pushes the woman.*
Below centre and right: *here the woman is using one of the postures of t'ai chi called 'Fan penetrates back' to raise the man's leading arm and push him in the chest, causing him to lose balance.*

T'AI CHI CHUAN

There are three recognized 'internal' martial arts of China: t'ai chi chuan, hsing-i and pakua, of which t'ai chi chuan is by far the most popular.

T'ai chi chuan means 'supreme ultimate fist'. The 'supreme ultimate' is one of the names given to the Yin-Yang symbol (see diagram above). The word fist is added to it because t'ai chi chuan has a martial side, although most people know of it as a form of gentle exercise. Its origins are obscure, but it is thought to have been practised for at least 5,000 years. Old Chinese drawings depict Taoist monks doing movements akin to t'ai chi – it was part of the study of their philosophy – and legends of the feats of t'ai chi masters abound. However, it is mainly thought of in connection with the calmness of mind and the restfulness of action which it brings to its followers. If the idea of restful action seems contradictory, then the sight of an elderly man or woman meandering through the sequences of movement of the art will explain the paradox. The movements are simultaneously beautiful, smooth, and even hypnotic. This last aspect may be due to the uninterrupted flow from one posture to another, giving the viewer no finished action on which to rest his gaze.

T'ai chi is unique; no other martial art has movements quite like it. It is also one of the most difficult to learn, in the sense that it takes a long time. The chief reason for this is the slowness of the movements and the circular actions involved. In karate, for instance, it takes time to develop power and timing, but the punching movement itself presents no problem. Also, karate movements are fast, and most people through their childhood and teenage experiences of sport are familiar with quick action. Reflex actions in which we catch a falling cup or pen are natural; they require no thinking. In t'ai chi movements are slowed down; students have to become aware of the body in a way which few other disciplines require. It is this slowing down and attention to the body which presents the problems. Some people find it irksome and uninteresting, but for those who respond it is an undying source of pleasure and self-knowledge.

There are various styles of t'ai chi. Over the centuries different masters modified the move-

ments and introduced ideas from other martial arts. Even so, the chief characteristics outlined above still remain in all of them. The style illustrated in this section is the Yang, named after the family who promulgated and preserved it. This is the most popular and most widely known style from the days prior to World War II. Since then the Chinese have introduced into their school and college curricula some modes of t'ai chi which begin at a simplified standard and proceed to long and complicated sequences of movement. There is, therefore, a pre- and post-revolutionary approach to the art: on the one hand there are the old forms with their Taoist connections and their ancient lore, and on the other there are the tradition-free forms of present-day China. The main difference is merely one of attitude. The same basic benefits can result from either approach.

The core of t'ai chi is the 'form': a series of postures, each with its own name such as 'White crane spreads its wings'. Although known as postures, they are never held in static form but are passed through as in ballet, where a whole series of pre-arranged positions make up a continuous dance. Forms vary in length from 18 postures to more than a hundred. Beginners are introduced to the idea of the form first, and are then taken through a few postures at each lesson. Over the centuries many variations of the movements have been introduced, but provided the principles are adhered to there is no need for the student to doubt the authenticity of what he is being taught.

People in almost every profession and walk of life find t'ai chi appealing, but actors and dancers in particular can learn something from the movement, and doctors and psychotherapists can find a source of relaxation for themselves and their patients. In connection with the latter, the medical side extends into Chinese medical theory through the term 'chi'. 'Chi' is the energy which Chinese physicians palpate when they take a patient's pulse. This universal energy is said to run throughout the human body, and the whole of nature; another word for it might be 'vitality'. Every organ has its own chi, and when the chi is balanced the human being is in a healthy condition. If there is too much or too little chi

somewhere in the body, then the balance is lost. The purpose of Chinese medicine is to balance the chi, and the study of t'ai chi is regarded as one of the self-help methods. Through slow, even movement the chi can be brought to a more stable condition. It should be pointed out, however, that it will take the student some time, depending on his ability and persistence, before this stage is reached.

At a later stage in t'ai chi training, or from the outset if it is the policy of the teacher, a student can take up the study of 'push hands'. Push hands is a form of training with a partner. The technique

Opposite page: *ideally, the tranquillity of meditation should also be found while performing the movements of t'ai chi.*

Above: *a transitional movement during the form. It is these movements, rather than the completed postures, which require the attention and help of a teacher.*

involves resting your hands on the arms of your partner and by moving your whole body gently pushing him back. He must learn first to give way or yield in a certain fashion, and then to push you back. The exercise develops into more complex forms of pushing and yielding, so that gradually the whole body becomes more sensitive to pressure. This can be an enjoyable experience and can also impart a great deal of self-knowledge to an alert student. One's habitual reactions to being pushed and losing balance are brought into focus and a kind of re-education begins.

Some schools of t'ai chi carry this study of push hands even further. The principle of yielding and pushing is extended into fighting modes, self-defence applications, and the application of concentrated 'chi' to deliver powerful 'pushes' and jarring shocks to an opponent's body. To explain how such a gentle art can be legitimately transformed in this way, let us take the analogy of water, a symbolic reference often found in Taoist writings and thought. When water in a river is deep and slow it

has one kind of power or energy, although it is not visually evident in any striking way. However, if this water is contained by a dam, and then suddenly released, the total thrust of millions of gallons projected through a narrow space will reveal a different kind of power, although the same substance is used.

In order to study and be effective in this use of t'ai chi, a long and difficult apprenticeship must be served. Part of the secret of eventual success is the ability to relax the body much more deeply than usual, but at the same time to have an acutely alert mind which can detect the right moment to 'strike'. In fact, all martial arts at their apex seek this sudden, well-timed and balanced application of force. Very few martial artists achieve it, but it is a goal worth aiming for; it is akin to the sudden enlightenment or 'satori' of Zen, or the moment of releasing the bow in Japanese archery.

Various weapons are used in t'ai chi. These include the double-edged sword, which is the favourite. In the West, however, weapons training is very rare.

Right: this is the 'Single whip' position of t'ai chi, with its characteristic 'beak' formation of the right hand fingers and thumb.
Below left: this position, occurring frequently in t'ai chi forms, is called 'Brush left knee and push'.
Below right: both students might be holding a guitar in this posture, so it is aptly named 'Play guitar'.
Bottom left: the students return to the 'Brush left knee and push' position.
Bottom right: the memorable name of this posture, with the right hand presented towards the ground, is 'Needle sticks at sea bottom'.
Opposite page: the posture 'Fan penetrates back' can be used to illustrate some important points about t'ai chi movement.

When the hand is raised, let the side of the chest below the arm 'open' or become free.

Even though the wrist is sometimes bent back, it should not be made tense as this is said to interrupt the flow of 'chi'.

When you perform a movement, remember what its practical application might be. Here for instance it might be catching a hand or stopping a blow to the head.

Do not let the open fingers become rigid.

When the arm is held out in front of the body keep the elbow down, not out to the side, and always slightly bent to avoid tension.

A flexible but firm waist movement is used in t'ai chi. When the waist moves, the trunk and arms move too.

A common fault among beginners is to raise the heel of the rear leg. Always keep the rear foot flat on the ground, even when it is not carrying much weight. In t'ai chi the weight is never evenly distributed on both feet.

The knee should follow the line of the foot; that is, it should be directly above it whenever possible. The knees are never fully straightened in t'ai chi, to avoid tension and to keep some potential movement in reserve.

When completing a movement, the rear foot is turned in towards the centre of the body, at an angle of 35 to 45 degrees. If this turning in movement is not performed, then the waist and trunk cannot turn completely either.

121

During the Sung dynasty, which lasted from AD 960–1279, a Chinese general, Yu Fei, distinguished himself in battle against the Kin tribes. He is credited with founding the martial art known as hsing-i or 'body-mind boxing'. There is no trace of hsing-i history for the next few hundred years, but during the Ming dynasty, 1368–1644, a book said to have been written by Yu Fei came to light and was given to a famous warrior, Chi Lung Feng. At this point a contradiction appears. On the one hand hsing-i is said to be based on spear movements and on the other on animal movements. The latter explanation is likely to be the more accurate; Feng's skill with the spear was well known and may have led to confusion.

Whatever the truth may be, modern hsing-i technique includes 12 animal forms or types of movement. However, the five basic actions are splitting, drilling, pounding, crossing and crushing. Combined with specific foot positions, they are ways of using the hands to parry and to strike an opponent. A student learns these movements alone before moving on to practise with a partner. The number five is significant in Chinese thinking

HSING-I CHUAN

This sequence shows a series of hsing-i stepping, blocking, kicking and punching movements, performed at high speed. It is used to close in on an opponent unexpectedly, with strength and power. The outstretched, open hand can be used to grip and pull as well as strike.

The distinctive leaping movements of hsing-i, by which a lot of ground is covered in a short time.

and it is no surprise to find it in such an ancient martial art. The five elements present in Chinese medical theory, geomancy, philosophy and so on are earth, fire, water, wood and metal. In hsing-i the five basic actions are related as follows: splitting corresponds to metal; drilling corresponds to water; pounding corresponds to fire; crossing corresponds to earth; and crushing corresponds to wood. Just as the five elements are related to one another, so the techniques of hsing-i have a definite technical relationship.

The Chinese character is essentially conservative. They do not easily discard cherished beliefs, even when new discoveries seem to contradict them. The five element theory was eventually questioned and found wanting, but it remained within the body of medical lore although the circulation of chi and the Yin-Yang theory (see page 117), as found in acupuncture, largely displaced it. In hsing-i the five basic actions also survived and are woven into the 12 styles of animal movements which are closely connected with the chi theory.

The animal forms are: dragon, tiger, horse, monkey, cock, turtle, hawk, swallow, snake, falcon, eagle and bear. Each animal form comprises a characteristic way of fighting and characteristic postures. Each posture stimulates or subdues the chi flowing through the ching-lo, the channels identified in acupuncture. For example, Douglas H. Y. Hsieh, a Chinese commentator on martial arts, points out that the tiger form depends on power from the back of the hips, a place where there is an important acupuncture point. It is also from this region of its body that the tiger is said to derive much of its leaping power. A feature of the hsing-i tiger form is the semi-squatting position, reminiscent perhaps of a tiger about to attack. At the other end of the scale is the swallow form, building up lightness and agility in the body. Variations on this form have been demonstrated in the West and are very graceful, as well as effective in combat.

The third section of hsing-i training deals with pre-arranged sparring methods carried out with a partner, in which each man knows in advance what his partner will do; it is a kind of martial arts choreography.

From the point of view of modern knowledge about the human body and its optimum functioning, hsing-i contains many other interesting features. For instance, it is scientifically proven that the relationship between the position of the head and the top of the spine plays an important part in good, natural breathing. It has also been shown that having the elbows slightly away from the body, palms turned out a little, similarly facilitates breathing. Both these points were strongly made by F. M. Alexander and Moshe Feldenkrais, whose work on human movement and movement therapy is now widely recognized. In the 800-year-old hsing-i style these same two points are important in the establishment of correct posture, being part of the eight fundamentals of stance and alertness.

These details, and many others, make the study of hsing-i a long-term affair. However, often the chief problem is to find an instructor. While teachers of the closely related t'ai chi abound, hsing-i teachers hang back from opening their doors to Western students. This is also true of pakua teachers (see page 126). It is common for Chinese t'ai chi instructors to have studied some hsing-i and pakua forms at some time in their careers, but they too are singularly reticent when it comes to teaching either of these arts. The reasons for this are not clear. Traditionally, all Chinese forms of fighting were jealously guarded by the family or clan to which they originally belonged. In former days this was understandable. An unknown style or technique could be a surprise to any potential enemy or challenger, so secrecy gave one the advantage. This practice has weakened in the second half of the twentieth century, but in a way that any beginner in martial arts should understand. If someone wishes to learn to swim or how to repair a car he or she can go to a teacher or club and be taught how to do it correctly. In the martial arts world, things are different. As interest in these ancient techniques grew in the West, the opportunity arose for martial artists to make money from teaching, and from appearing in films and writing books. Some began to teach openly, holding nothing back from their students. Others spun out their sharing of information over an intolerably long period, and students left before they had learned the inner secrets of the art. Still others taught their students incorrectly, on purpose, leaving out the small points which make the difference between success and failure. A fourth group set themselves up as experts but were not. All kinds of variations on these four categories of teacher exist, so Western students should look at martial arts training critically at all times. With experience one acquires a capacity to sum up the situation with speed.

Secrecy was paramount during the time of the warrior Chi Lung Feng, and one of his students, Ma Hsieh Li, learned from him initially in a way that is found in several histories of martial arts styles. Ma spied on his teacher as he practised his art, then went away and trained from what he remembered. Ma's apparently underhand methods were revealed, but far from upbraiding him, Chi Lung Feng accepted him formally as a student. The art was passed onto several others before it was learned by Li Lao Nan. In middle age he began to teach hsing-i more openly in his native province of Hopei, and it is mainly due to him that the general public were made aware of the power of hsing-i. In the twentieth century another hsing-i expert, Wang Hsiang Jeh, is known to have defeated a Japanese swordsman in a contest, using only a wooden cudgel. He explained that his weapon was merely an extension of his hand, and that as he was superior to his challenger in empty-hand combat he was also superior to him with weapons.

In recent times the martial arts writer Robert Smith has recounted how John Bluming, amateur judo champion in the Netherlands and one of the strongest Western karate men ever to train in Japan, actually injured his wrist testing hsing-i expert Wang Shu-chin's ability to withstand the most powerful blows to the abdomen or solar plexus. When Bluming asked, a little put out and wanting to find some way of getting back at Wang, 'What else can he do?', he was at once invited to take a 'punch' from the hsing-i man. Wang rested his fingers on Bluming's stomach, curled them into a fist and screwed his fist inwards. Bluming was bent over in agony and has since been 'a believer'. The training of hsing-i students to gain this type of power is similar to that endured by hard-style qigong practitioners (see wushu, page 132). Wang told Smith that the students of a famous Beijing master would stand in the freezing snow for up to six hours practising hsing-i breathing methods.

Such rigorous training may not be required by all the modern hsing-i masters, but it is nevertheless a demanding art which can be taken up by anyone of reasonable fitness under the age of 40. To be able to perform all the 12 animal styles and the five basic actions requires a wide range of skills that take time to develop. Each animal's special quality must be displayed. To perform with the lightness of a swallow, the might of a tiger and the grandeur of the mysterious dragon is no small undertaking, but getting there can be a satisfying journey.

PAKUA

Above and opposite: this sequence shows a pakua student 'walking the circle', with the highly distinctive palm positions, body turning and foot positions clearly in evidence. The eyes and the palms work in close harmony.

126

'Looks like a woman, fights like a tiger' is a saying dear to the hearts of teachers of the Chinese internal or 'soft' arts. Paul Kuo, a master of pakua, used similar but stronger imagery to sum up his art: 'Like a lady dancing, and in a fight, like a tiger.'

Training in pakua (pronounced ba-gua) consists of learning to walk in a circle, changing direction while twining the arms in a specific way, and walking back along the same circumference. This patience-testing, and to some students boring, exercise is connected with the eight trigrams. A trigram is a series of horizontal lines, one on top of the other. An unbroken line is a 'strong' line, a Yang or masculine line, and a line broken into two equal halves is a 'weak' line, a Yin or feminine line.

In the I-Ching classic, *The Book of Changes,* the trigrams in many combinations are seen as a guide to action, a method of divination. Books on the theory of pakua show combinations of eight trigrams placed in a circle, denoting the eight points of the compass. As a student walks the circle he passes these eight points and should carefully consider the qualities and directions he is meeting and leaving behind. In fact, very few students of pakua are mindful of the eight trigrams theory during training. Although it gives its name to the style, the complexities and mental effort involved in exploring it in practice are beyond them. The ramifications of meaning of the trigrams are such that Confucius said he would have liked to have lived

another 40 years simply to be able to study them further. Paul Kuo said that he walked the circle simply relaxing, concentrating and feeling. That is probably enough for most people.

The origins of pakua are not known. It was only in 1796 that a kung fu teacher turned up in Shantung province and gave some lessons to a student called Feng Ke-shan, from whom a line is traceable to the present day. As in several other kung fu styles, the traditional story is that pakua was founded by a Taoist monk. Since the dominant theme of the art is the circle, it follows that pakua students do not meet force with force, but try to deflect it. The continuous circle also means that on the one hand the student has the possibility of falling asleep, while on the other hand he has the possibility of waking up. That is, the apparent simplicity of the action enables his mind, his attention, to come back into his body, to reinforce his powers of alert observation, and as Paul Kuo said, to concentrate and to feel. What he endeavours to feel his way towards is the right posture; he should be as erect as a column of smoke on a still day, but also relaxed. Gradually his attention is focused more inwardly, and the possibilities inherent in pakua become clearer.

Purists maintain that pakua has no techniques except the single and double palm changes – the correct name for the intertwining arm movements. The increased sensitivity and awareness which

8   9   10   11

come from training produce the right action at the right moment. This high aim has not satisfied everyone, possibly because it is too difficult. What has happened is that different masters and clubs have produced their own techniques and many have become standard pakua methods. This is contrary to the spirit of the art, lowering it to a more mechanical level, and should be resisted. The possibilities inherent in the circle are infinite, and with a little imagination can be explored, even without studying pakua at all.

Imagine that two men appear on the scene. Man A stands still, while man B walks in a circle around him. Man A can attack man B along any radius of the circle, but B can evade A by continuing to walk or he can turn on his heels and go back the opposite way. B keeps his hands up in front of his body, protecting his abdomen and groin, chest and face. He keeps his body slightly turned in towards A at all times. If A attacks, B needs to keep moving his hands to protect his body and to do this he uses the single or double palm changes. A's attack may be so sudden and strong that B cannot merely continue to walk out of the way. He needs to resort to an even sharper change of direction, cutting into the circle at an angle to avoid the attack. If the attack is high up on his body he may have to dip down; if it is low, he may have to rise. Once he leaves the plane of the circle he is entering into a sphere of movement; some martial arts writers have called this the dynamic sphere.

The reference to the dancing lady gives an indication of the possible grace of movement inherent in circular action, and underlines the apparent ease of manner of the pakua circle walker.

However, when he strikes, the pakua student becomes a tiger and is ferocity itself; since no rules are laid down concerning what manner of attack or defence he may use, no part of the anatomy is out of bounds.

Several famous masters of other styles have admitted that of all the opponents they might face, those of the eight trigram school fill them with the most misgivings. Traditionally, kung fu contests were staged formally in front of a crowd, or else a student from one style might enter the training hall of another style and issue a challenge. If one of the contestants were a pakua man, his opponent would not know what to expect, except that there would be some type of evasion, and any type of counter-attack.

In pakua the palms are most often used in striking techniques. To Westerners this may come as a surprise as we associate the palms with a slap, and the clenched fist with a punch. A fist seems tougher, as it presents the knuckle bones, and it gives a slightly longer reach. On the other hand, the fist is more easily damaged if it hits bone, while the heel of the palm is cushioned by muscle. The force of the fist has to be carried through the wrist and palm joints, while the palm is on the 'end' of the arm and transmits the full force of the arm rather like the thrust of a short staff. A palm strike can also be turned into a grab or claw-like grip, whereby the attacker can hold on to his opponent's flesh or a nerve point, while a fist is shut tight. Consequently, many kung fu stylists prefer to use striking techniques involving the palms rather than the fists.

No special standard of physical fitness is needed to begin to walk the circle. However, expert teachers of this powerful, evasive art are not easy to find in the West at the present time.

Opposite page, above left: the man on the right blocks a punch with a high, open palm position.

Opposite page, above right: with a similar technique he turns his partner away, 'revealing' his back.

Opposite page, below left: he can now punch his partner's rib cage.

Opposite page, below right: he follows this up with a second punch.

Above left: in the 'ready' position.

Above: the man on the right moves in to kick.

Left: the kick comes in, but the defender catches the attacker's foot in his arm.

Below left: the attacker is turned over and down.

Below: in this position he is very vulnerable to a counterattack.

WUSHU

In Chinese wushu the fighting arts of kung fu are transformed into martial athletics. After the Communist revolution in 1949, a big effort was made to 'sift through the old to bring forth the new'. The leadership wanted to preserve what was useful in the reactionary traditional martial arts of China. Experts scrutinized many styles and collated an immense body of techniques, creating an extensive educational syllabus. Today, this syllabus is widely taught in China and in many overseas countries. Two international wushu competitions have been held in China, in which athletes were judged on the excellence of their techniques, and although the Chinese have shown that they are far superior to foreign entrants, the West is catching up.

Wushu is a word from the Mandarin dialect, while kung fu is a Cantonese expression. Wushu was originally the formal name for combative martial arts and kung fu was more colloquial. In the post-revolutionary Chinese mind, the expression kung fu is associated with much that is distasteful: mystical beliefs, a hierarchical society, despotic warlords, agricultural servitude, capitalism, and so forth. Communist spokesmen and writers openly condemn old-style kung fu as useless in the face of modern weaponry. The new concept of wushu as an athletic syllabus, raising the standard of the nation's health, serves the two-fold purpose of falling in line with Communist thinking and preserving part of China's cultural heritage.

The northern styles of wushu were particularly athletic in their pre-revolutionary forms and they have been extensively used in creating the new

Wushu's classical double-edged straight sword shown in combination with a leaping action, sword arm balanced by the outstretched rear arm.

syllabus. Their spectacular kicks are said to have contributed to the techniques of Korean taekwondo (see page 166), dating from the time when Korea was a Chinese colony. In 1974 the grace and acrobatic skills of a Chinese wushu troupe thrilled American audiences for the first time and helped to signal the new detente between the United States and China. Since that time, many visits have been made by Chinese wushu groups to all parts of the world, to promote a sporting art which China hopes to see included in future Olympic Games.

The wushu spirit is one of friendship and excellence. In the early decades of the twentieth century the Western attitude to sport, with its emphasis on winning, reached China and grew in popularity until Mao Tse-tung threw out such ideas. The slogan 'friendship first' emerged from his ideological purge and still pertains, which is a tribute to Chinese tenacity in the face of world sporting pressures. It remains to be seen, should wushu gain a place in the Olympics, if this non-competitive spirit can survive.

In addition to many empty-hand, unarmed systems, part of the heritage of wushu is the use of classical weapons. Some are bizarre, others are beautiful. They include the big chopper, a kind of halberd with a very short handle and an immense blade; the steel whip, composed of short pieces of chain-linked metal; the tasselled spear; the staff and the three-sectional staff; the scimitar-shaped sword or big knife; the straight, double-edged classical sword; and the double-ended dagger. Modified, display weapons are used so that no real harm can come to the participants. In the past, weapons masters, particularly swordsmen, always had some magical, mystical quality; they could virtually fly! They fly no more, but they have been replaced by men and women whose fitness, agility and flexibility are truly amazing.

Westerners can rarely emulate the grace which the Chinese bring to their wushu. Show an untrained Chinese, unspoiled by any other physical discipline or movements system, some techniques of wushu and he or she will perform them with an indefinable quality which even an advanced Western pupil will be unable to equal. However, Western women do seem to have a similar feeling for wushu in some cases, and indeed wherever wushu is performed women students are prominent. Even in the most powerfully executed wushu movement there is an element of softness, perhaps due to a deep sense of relaxation, and it may be that women are more in touch with this experience than men.

The most recent indications from China are that much of the rejected material associated with old-style kung fu is being allowed back into the wushu syllabus. The new tolerance is even more apparent in the acceptance of 'chi kung' or 'qigong', which comprises a large body of traditional exercises and breathing techniques used in modern China chiefly for medical rehabilitation purposes.

Chinese thinking about human health and behaviour has always had the concept of 'chi' behind it (see t'ai chi, page 116). In Japanese it is translated as 'ki', as in ai-ki-do (see page 24). This 'chi' or vitality must also be present in wushu performance. It is an element which lifts a mere movement into an aesthetic action and evidence of its presence is looked for by the judge when he allots a score to a competitor. Wushu experts who split rocks, bricks or ice in demonstrations also attribute their skill to their ability to focus the chi in their bodies. A photograph which often appears in martial arts magazines shows a thin, elderly man slapping a pile of bricks. This strange character could, so it is reported, break any brick in the pile simply with a slap. The slap he gave was not the kind one gives a naughty child. It came from the iron palm tradition, in which students initially toughen their hands, but later learn the recondite techniques of properly directed hitting.

An example of a modern, formalized group of wushu movements containing many pre-revolutionary actions and ideas is the chang chuan 'A-level' set, made known in the West by Michael P. Staples and Anthony K. Chan. Chang chuan means 'long fist'; its techniques develop power in the waist and shoulders, and improve balance and technical precision. In keeping with Chinese tradition, chang chuan acknowledges that one is performing on the earth, and that the earth has four major compass points. These compass points are conspicuous in the ancient Chinese art of geomancy, in which one relates one's activities to the invisible energies, the chi, of the planet itself. Chang chuan has eight sections. As in most wushu series of movements, the set is begun facing towards the auspicious south, the direction of warmth and prosperity. From then on, the odd-numbered sections of the set are performed to the east and the even-numbered to the west. The north is a direction of cold and is inauspicious for wushu.

The set begins with powerful arm movements, knee bends in which the performer assumes what is known as the horse-riding stance, and upward-turning leaps. Jumping kicks are soon introduced and are combined with the strong arm movements. Next come low, stretching stances followed by more high leaps and kicks. The set culminates in low, bending, sweeping arm movements, one complete

*Above left: the first in a series of
movements from the chang chuan set,
from a modern wushu syllabus.
Above right: the student prepares to
leap up.*

*Below: he leaps high, both arms
thrown back in preparation for an
attacking descent.*

Above left: as he lands he sinks into a low stance with simultaneous high and low arm movements.
Above right: he turns into a similar position on the other side.

Below left: he transfers most of his weight onto his left leg.
Below right: he thrusts forward with his open left palm.

Above left: *a striking posture, arms flung wide apart and back, resembling a bird in flight.*
Above right: *training in pairs. These students show the use of low wushu stances.*

Below: *a high leaping kick with a partner who displays a classical wushu defensive stance.*

Above: as the man on the left attacks with a
downward strike, using the staff, his partner
demonstrates a block using the three-sectional staff.

somersault and a gradual return to movements
similar to those carried out at the start. Many of
these actions would be useless in combat, since they
are stylized versions of the original techniques. The
chang chuan set therefore illustrates the athletic
rather than the martial nature of wushu. A wide
range of athletic, even gymnastic, skills are required
and are usually developed in wushu classes.

In China, school children, factory workers,
university students and many others perform
wushu routines on a regular basis. Young girls and
boys begin with the most basic movements and if
they show promise may be taken under the wing
of one of the wushu governing bodies, with the
possibility of graduating into the demonstration
teams which tour the world. Wushu movements
also appear in modern Beijing Opera, which features a wide range of martial arts skills. Here wushu
merges with acrobatics and juggling, requiring a
level of physical dexterity peculiar to the Chinese.

In team wushu, training to produce the brilliant movements is severe. Effortlessness is seen
to grow from discipline, and wushu coaches are
constantly at work refining and improving performance. Unlike many of the traditional martial

arts, wushu does not stand still; it has not crystallized into invariable sequences of techniques. An
example of this can be seen in the wushu system
known as combined t'ai chi chuan, created by the
Chinese National Athletic Committee. This is an
advanced form of t'ai chi, combining several different styles. In the words of the famous wushu
teacher Madame Bow Sim Mark, it contains the
'hard and soft [movements] of Chen style, the open
elegance of the peaceful Yeung style, the light and
swift movements of the Sun style, the compactness
of Wu style and the total balance of Fu style'. In
addition, a beginner's form was produced called
the 24-step Beijing form, or simplifed t'ai chi. It
would, however, be a tremendous pity if the original old systems mentioned by Madame Bow Sim
Mark were to disappear, as each has its characteristic mood and tempo which, with the best will in
the world, the combined form cannot be said to
encompass entirely.

The training of the men who break bricks and
allow hammers to be slammed into boards lying
across their unprotected bodies is more of a mystery.
This aspect of wushu is connected with qigong
(chee-gung is the nearest pronunciation), the art of
directing internal energy or chi and focusing it on
any internal area of the body or external object, and
ever since the 1970s, when a 50-year-old Chinese,
Hou Shuying, broke a granite slab using his head

Above: *a downward attack with the staff is blocked by a cross defence using the three-sectional staff.*

Below: *a low attack from a three-sectional staff is avoided by an acrobatic leap and downward counter.*

during a wushu demonstration in San Francisco, the martial arts world has not stopped talking about it. According to the two writers mentioned earlier, Staples and Chan, training in qigong to break objects does not belong solely in the realm of mystical meditation. At the tender age of seven, Hou became a pupil of an elderly monk called Huayin, a master of hard-style qigong. Performing exercises which would have horrified any Western parent, Hou climbed the ladder of qigong techniques, learning how to regulate his breathing and 'swallow his breath'. Having reached puberty, he remained celibate for many years, waking regularly at midnight to bang his head some 300 times against a wall. This amazing regime did not concuss him or cause brain damage. From 1945–52 he was in the army, but never broke from his rigorous training. He did marry later and suffered no apparent loss of ability. (Some schools of qigong consider that proficiency in the art requires sexual abstinence.)

Athletic wushu and the qigong demonstrations which accompany it are incompatible, says Hou, since 'there isn't enough time to learn both'. His three sons and one daughter have followed in their father's footsteps. When Hou says that the reasons for studying qigong today are 'to promote health and clarity of mind', one cannot forego a faint smile as one thinks of his head meeting the granite.

Qigong is also used as a healing art. In Beijing and Hong Kong there are schools that teach how to generate healing energy in the palms; this energy can be transmitted to the bodies of patients, especially those suffering from the type of illness which responds most dramatically to acupuncture: arthritis, neurasthenia, stomach complaints caused by a high degree of nervousness, and a whole range of ailments which in the West are described as psychosomatic.

Wushu offers a unique opportunity. Anyone who decides to join a class can enjoy its modern athletic emphasis (the qigong aspects are rarely taught in the West), while being part of China's ancient martial arts history.

Top: a strong, forward thrusting attack with the double-edged straight sword.
Centre: a low stance using the curved sword. The front and rear arms balance one another.
Bottom: a single-arm 'cartwheel', combined with a movement of the double-edged straight sword. Weapons and acrobatic skills go together in wushu.

The twin Wing Chun butterfly knives displayed in a powerful, two-handed, simultaneous attack (left hand) and defensive movement (right hand).

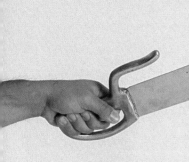

WING CHUN KUNG FU

This Chinese martial art is the most widely known but the least spectacular; the most controversial yet in many ways the simplest; the most written about but frequently the most misunderstood. Why has it received so much attention? Bruce Lee studied it.

Bruce Lee's meteoric rise to fame in the 1970s and his sudden and unexplained death left behind a glowing trail. Part of this trail was made up of the Wing Chun style of kung fu, which Lee had studied for a while in his native Hong Kong under the direction of its Chinese grandmaster, Yip Man. According to the grandmaster's son, Master Yip Chun, the traditionally brought up Yip Man and the more westernized Bruce Lee eventually came to a parting of the ways, mainly because Lee chose, when he visited the United States, to teach the Americans the Wing Chun techniques he had learned so far; until that time this particular martial art had been practised exclusively by the Chinese.

During the late 1960s and early 1970s several books on Wing Chun were published in English, and Chinese teachers of varying standards began to teach Westerners; the cat was really out of the bag. The Bruce Lee films, in which the screen hero demolished all comers with contemptuous and spectacular ease, ironically did not display Lee's Wing Chun skills primarily, but featured more cinematically appealing techniques, especially kicks, which Lee had learned from taekwondo experts in the United States, as well as from other stylists.

In spite of the furore caused by the forbidden doors of Wing Chun being opened to the West, Wing Chun teachers stressed the connection between their art and Lee, while at the same time criticizing Lee for being the key figure in bringing about the change. Wing Chun kwoons (the Chinese word for training halls) bulged with new recruits, all wishing to learn the skills displayed by the kung fu superstar. Even more ironically, these fans did not realize that their hero had never learned the complete Wing Chun system, and that the true heirs of Grandmaster Yip Man were still living in comparative obscurity. It was only much later, after Lee's death, that the names of teachers such as

William Cheung, Leung Ting and Yip Chun came to the fore. After almost 20 years the personal rivalries, claims and counterclaims, concerning who is the most direct descendant, technically speaking, of Grandmaster Yip Man, have died down, and the style has found a leading place in the array of kung fu systems which may be studied.

An important footnote is needed here. Lee's encounters with other martial arts and with many Americans who were on the whole much bigger and heavier than the Hong Kong Chinese, led him to the decision that he needed a wider range of techniques. With the help of fellow martial artists he produced, after much research and experimentation, his own style known as jeet kune do – the Way of the Intercepting Fist. One of his best-known pupils during this period was Dan Inosanto, a teacher of escrima (see page 150), who also taught Lee something of his own Filipino art. Lee finally came to the conclusion that much of the traditional martial arts training was a 'classical mess', outdated, repetitive, and frequently full of methods which had no real fighting value. He came to believe chiefly in spontaneity of reaction and the use of any technique, including split-second inspiration, provided that it was effective. Interestingly, this simplicity of outlook corresponds with the basic theory of Wing Chun fighting, underlying a third irony: that in a sense Lee stayed close to the art which he had left behind.

The principal theme of Wing Chun is simplicity. An imaginary 'centre line' is drawn vertically through a standing man. All attacks are aimed at this central area, and all defences concentrate on defending it. Because of this, defensive arm movements need not stray beyond the shoulders or the hips, since these points mark the limits of attack. Attacking punches are delivered in a straight line, using a lot of elbow force. Heavy swings assisted by big body movements or forward lunges, such as one finds in Western boxing, are eliminated.

Wing Chun training is divided into three levels. The first level, siu lim tao, consists of standing still in a narrow horse-riding stance, and practising the basic punches, parries and blocks. To an outsider these look mystifying until their application is shown, and then they are seen as simple, economical and effective movements. The second level, chum kil, emphasizes defensive movements, turning the body and delivering low kicks. Chinese martial arts are roughly divided into northern and southern systems, and Wing Chun, a southern system, characteristically has only a few kicks, mainly aimed at the lower part of the body. The third level, bil jee, concentrates on open-handed finger attacks, combined with simultaneous defensive and attacking moves. In Wing Chun, as distinct from many other martial arts, defensive and offensive moves are always carried out at the same time. For example, a block is made with the left hand while the right hand delivers a punch. Or, a punching block may be used in which the blocking or parrying arm turns into a punching arm. The three levels are performed alone, and they correspond to what in karate and several other

arts is called a kata – a pre-arranged form or series of movements. In kung fu a kata is often referred to in translation as a 'set', meaning a set pattern of movements.

Training in the three levels can take years or months, depending on the teacher. Soon after training begins, students start to work with a partner on what is called chi sao or 'sticking hands'. In this exercise student A takes up a defensive position with one hand and an offensive position with the other hand. Student B does the same with opposite

A typical posture using the long Wing Chun pole. Note that the grip is close to one end, requiring considerable strength.

The 'centre line' running through the body shows the main target area for *Wing Chun* attacks.

Fists are held along the centre line, ready to punch or block.

One fist (or open hand) is kept behind the other, as a back-up for punching or blocking.

Elbows are lowered to protect the trunk, whenever possible.

Shoulders are kept down, not hunched.

The hands can drop instantly to defend the groin area.

143

hands and the two place both arms in contact with one another. Keeping this contact, A tries to punch B while B defends; at the same time B tries to punch A while A defends. There is a pattern to this exercise which students learn, and the training is designed to give experience in close-range fighting and sticking, i.e. remaining in contact with an opponent and driving through into his centre line. This exercise, which amounts to a lightning game of martial arts chess, also builds up the arms. No strong contact must be made by either man, should his attacking punch get through the other's defences.

Later on, students can practise their fighting techniques wearing special armour, gloves and headguards. Protected in this way, they can punch,

kick and block much harder.

These training methods are used in all Wing Chun clubs. There are many additional attack and defence techniques which may be taught, employing the full range of Wing Chun moves. Also, there is training on a wooden dummy, which consists of a thick cylinder of wood with one low wooden leg and three wooden arms projecting at different angles and levels. This training aid helps students to study their combined attacking and defensive moves and toughens up the arms and legs. Once again there is a set form to be performed on the dummy, consisting of 108 movements. However, the number varies depending on the teacher and the depth of his knowledge.

The chief weapons of Wing Chun are the

This sequence shows movements from the three sets or training forms of Wing Chun. The first two (left to right) are from siu lim tao, the next two are from chum kil, and the last two are from bil jee. Punching, blocking, kicking and striking with the fingers are featured.

butterfly knives, which are always used in pairs, and the long pole. Although there are several forms peculiar to the knives, many of the empty-hand forms of the art can be performed holding these weapons. The pole may be up to 4 metres long and is quite heavy. As it is held at one end, it is extremely hard to control. For an expert, one of its principal uses might be to clear a room of intruders, who could be kept at a safe distance from the holder of the weapon.

What is probably a unique feature of Wing Chun is the 'three to one inch punch', made famous by Lee. The principal punch of the system is made with a clenched fist held vertically, with the back of the hand at right angles to the floor. As the fist lands, propelled by strong elbow action, it turns upwards

and moves back towards the forearm. With diligent effort this final wrist flexion can be given considerable power, and at demonstrations Wing Chun teachers often show their ability to deliver strong blows from a distance of no more than 'three to one inches' from a person's body, sending him reeling backwards.

Wing Chun history begins at the Shaolin Temple in Honan province, where the famed Bodhidharma (AD 448–527), founder of Ch'an Buddhism (Zen), resided. Over the centuries this temple was destroyed and rebuilt many times, but it was always a centre of martial arts activity. At first, fighting methods based on animal movements were taught there: dragon style, tiger style, leopard style, snake style and crane style. Each of these

Above left: ready to begin sparring.
Above right: as the attacker on the right moves in, the defender parries his blows.

Below left: the defender (left) counters with a punch to the face, at the same time stepping in with his left leg behind the attacker's right leg.
Below right: the defender brings his left leg up behind the attacker's thigh, striking him off balance with his left arm and gripping the attacker's right arm with his right hand.

Above: a three-fold action – pulling with one hand, sweeping back with the left arm and forward with the left leg – completely upsets the attacker.

Above: the attacker is powerless. He may be dropped to the floor or struck in a number of ways.

animals was related to a particular human trait. The dragon corresponded to spirit; the tiger corresponded to bones; the leopard corresponded to power; the snake corresponded to breath; and the crane corresponded to energy. Later, other martial arts styles were added, forms were changed or improved, and exercise systems were introduced. In the seventeenth century the hated Manchu conquered China, putting an end to the Ming dynasty, and under their rule the Shaolin Temple became one of the centres for plots to overthrow the government: 'Destroy the Ch'ing [Manchu], restore the Ming.' Manchurian clothing was imposed on the people, together with a shaven head and the growing of the 'queue' or pigtail.

The energetic monks of the temple began to teach people their fighting arts. Word of this reached the Manchu emperor and he passed a law forbidding the practice of martial arts. Ignoring this decree, the monks trained in the early morning to avoid detection, a tradition observed out of respect to this day. The prohibition was made in 1729, but by 1735 the emperor still suspected the monks of

revolutionary activities and decided to approach the problem in a different way. He ordered the governor of Honan to pull down the temple and then rebuild it in such a way that no secret activities could take place there, as at that time it had many concealed areas. Finally it was decided that the temple should be demolished altogether, and the army was sent in. After many attempts, the temple was razed to the ground and only five inmates managed to escape with their lives. The fall of the temple had in fact been brought about by a Shaolin renegade monk, Ma Ling Er, who had been disciplined for breaking an ancient lamp, and in resentment had deserted to the Manchu army, giving them secret details of the temple complex.

The surviving inmates, Ng Mui, Pak Mee, Fung Do Tak, Miao Hin and Gee Sin, were known as the Venerable Five. Ng Mui was a nun who possessed great boxing skills. She took refuge in the Green Temple on White Crane mountain, and there met a young girl, Yim Wing Chun, to whom she passed on her knowledge of kung fu. Yim Wing Chun in turn taught her husband and the pair later learned the knife techniques from the daughter of another of the Venerable Five. The empty-hand and knife techniques were passed from one person to another and were finally taught to Leung Yee Tye, an actor in an opera troupe. The troupe's cook was none other than Gee Sin, a master of the pole techniques, and he taught Leung his particular skill. So it was that three out of the Venerable Five contributed to the Wing Chun kung fu repertoire. Leung Yee Tye taught Leung Tsan, who taught Chan Wah Soon. Chan had only 16 pupils, one of whom was Yip Man. Thus students of this martial art are heirs to a long and fascinating history.

You do not need to be strong to study Wing Chun. It is based on speed and economy of movement rather than on muscular strength. The greatest stress falls on the arms and shoulders. It is a fighting system par excellence, with many good self-defence techniques. However, it is only when the second or better still the third level has been absorbed, and progression has been made from the static early training positions into a dynamic mode, that one can say one is equipped to deal with a one-to-one real-life emergency. The only arguable criticism of Wing Chun as a complete fighting art is that it may be vulnerable to heavy, charging attacks which could result in loss of balance.

Opposite page, above: *ready for chi sao or 'sticking hands' training.*
Above left: *the man on the left punches and his partner parries.*
Above: *the situation is reversed.*
Opposite page, far left: *the man on the left thrusts and his partner parries.*
Opposite page, left: *as the punching, parrying and thrusting continue, the arms and hands of the partners continue to 'stick' or remain in contact, defending the centre line.*
Left: *an example of the four-fold simultaneous movements of chi sao. The man on the left attacks low with his right arm, which his partner parries with his left arm. At the same time, the man on the right attacks high with his right arm, which his partner parries with his left arm.*

ESCRIMA

By a strange twist of fate, kung fu film star Bruce Lee was instrumental in popularizing the fighting arts of the Philippines in the West. This came about through Lee's friendship with Daniel Inosanto. Inosanto studied Lee's own kung fu system, jeet kune do, and also taught the star some of the stick and empty-hand methods of escrima. These were featured in some of Lee's films and also gradually became incorporated into the repertoire of jeet kune do. Other teachers of escrima, such as Rene Latosa, came to Europe, but without the impetus of its association with Lee it is doubtful that the art would have become as popular as it has.

There are many people of Philippine descent living in the United States but they, and the inhabitants of the islands themselves, kept their art secret until the rise in interest in the West more or less forced them to disclose some of the techniques. Escrima, and its sister arts, kali and arnis de mano, first came to Western attention early in the sixteenth century when the Spanish invaded the Philippines and banned all training in martial arts. This did not prevent the conquered people from disguising their art and practising it in the form of stage plays, known as 'moro-moro', the climax of which was often a mock battle with blades of some kind. The arnis de mano expression is said to have come from the Spanish description of the leather harnesses used by the moro-moro actors, the correct word 'arnes' being corrupted to arnis. A mistaken idea that the Spaniards brought escrima to the conquered islands sprang up at that time and has persisted to this day, in spite of rebuttals. The other name, kali, refers to blades in general, and although among purists a distinction is made between the art of kali and that of escrima and arnis de mano, the term escrima is commonly used to mean all the Philippine martial arts taught in the West today.

Because of the widespread violence in the world, escrima instruction tends to be limited to the use of sticks and empty-hand techniques. But, as every escrima student knows, a stick technique can represent a knife or long-bladed technique, so any attempt on the part of well-meaning authorities to banish knives from the scene is, from a technical point of view, futile.

An interesting point has been made by students of martial arts about the relationship between weapons and the climate and clothing of people who practise them. In parts of the world where the climate is hot and clothing light or scanty, the need for heavy weapons which can penetrate heavy clothing does not exist. A short, light weapon could damage a lightly clad person quite easily. This point may not stand up to rigorous, universal scrutiny, but it is worth considering. The Philippine climate is hot and the people lightly clad; the knife is sufficient. Also, a knife can be concealed in the clothing but easily reached, and escrima is essentially an art of stealth, subterfuge and such fast action that the art of fixing the eyes and not blinking during an encounter is taught in many schools. A blink could mean death.

Knife size and shape as well as stick length varies. The sticks shown on these pages are the length and thickness used in westernized training. As in all martial arts using weapons described in this book, the social conditions in the West do not require or permit the practical use of such weapons, therefore all of them are in a sense 'arts' or, to borrow the Japanese expression, 'do' or 'ways'. To encourage the study of these arts, most of them have developed a sporting, competitive side, and escrima is no exception. During the 1980s Point Escrima was devised, with a prescribed fighting area, a scoring system, body armour in many cases and national competitions. By such means, some of the pressure and tension of a real situation could be simulated. But, as some strict commentators on martial arts have pointed out, citing kendo (see page 42) as an example, a definite distinction should be made between these sporting affairs and real combat. In sport, techniques are allowed and risks are taken which would not be countenanced in training for warfare.

In escrima the prime target is never a vital part of the body. The reason for this is that if a man armed with a blade managed to strike a vital spot, the training and reflexes of the injured man would enable him to cut or stab his attacker, possibly inflicting an equal amount of damage. The prime target is therefore the hand or the lower part of the arm that is carrying the weapon. A disarmed man is much less dangerous. In Daniel Inosanto's approach to escrima, he often teaches different methods of disarming. Similarly, when Rene Latosa first arrived in Europe, students expected him to teach methods of attacking the body with the sticks. He smiled warmly and began to teach them how to attack the hands and arms, and disarming tactics.

Astonishing stories are told of the American

A selection of techniques recognized as scoring strokes in escrima contests.
Above left: a descending stick stroke to the head.
Above right: a thrusting stick technique.

Below left: a low leg stroke technique.
Below right: a middle body stroke.

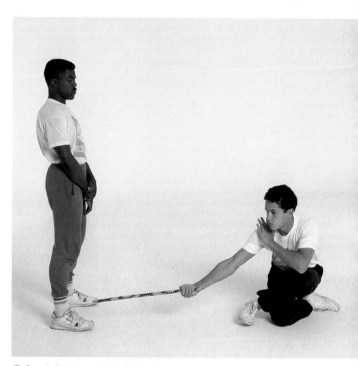

Above left: the attacker prepares to
drop low by taking his right leg back.

Above right: at ground level he may
attack the knees and ankles of his partner.

Below left: the attacker is beginning
to lower his position.

Below right: the attacker reaches a
low, half-kneeling position to strike at
the middle region of his partner's body.

occupation of the Philippines in the late nineteenth century. There was much bloodshed, as the Filipinos did not welcome the Americans any more warmly than they had the Spaniards. There was also a high degree of religious fervour attached to this resentment as most of the inhabitants fighting the Americans were Muslims. On more than one occasion a Muslim fanatic donned a red headband as a sign that he would not stop killing until he himself was killed. Then, armed with a blade, he ran amok. The army issue .38 hand gun was found to be too light a weapon to deal with such men. It was known for the .38 to be fired until empty into the body of a man running amok and he would still manage to strike the soldier armed with the gun. This led to the issue of the heavier .45 hand gun with much more stopping power. These events underline the basic escrima policy of disarming a man first. In an ideal situation, the man with the gun would have shot his attacker in the hand or fist, knocking the knife out of his grasp.

Such bloody events have nothing to do with Western escrima training, but they indicate the sound reasoning which lies behind the technical aspects of the art. A new student begins by learning how to hold and use a stick. In the soundest type of school he would be discouraged from twirling the stick or holding it with the smallest and third finger loose. The best grip for fighting is a firm hold with the thumb and four fingers. This helps to ensure that the weapon is not easily knocked from the hand. Mobility comes from the use of the wrist, combined with the elbow and shoulder. 'Body shifting' – the art of moving in on an opponent or getting out of his way – is a vital aspect of escrima which must be cultivated by the student, along with a sense of timing and distance. It is of great importance to know how far away you are from your opponent, how far his stick will reach, how fast he can move, and how quickly he can approach or remove himself from the scene. These instincts, which in the West do not need to be highly developed, may be a matter of life and death in more primitive societies.

Students who have studied Japanese martial arts and then move on to escrima may find the approach to training frustrating. This is because Japanese martial arts are so formal; everything is laid down. In escrima it is also laid down, but in a different way. The student is taught long-range, medium-range and close-range fighting, but he is taught to react in a way that seems 'natural' to him; he is meant to 'feel' what is right. Thus a kind of tension develops between the Western urge to know, to explain, to figure it all out beforehand, and the almost instinctive knowledge of the native Filipino of what feels right.

Although various systems of escrima are taught in the West, an exploration of one of them will give those interested in taking up the art a general idea. A stick is firmly held close to the end, and wrist exercises to improve flexibility are introduced. Five target areas are designated – the upper right and left sides of the body, the lower left and right sides, and the centre line – and training in strikes to the first four and thrusts at the centre line begun. Footwork is triangular. Attacking or defending, an escrima student steps along one of the sides of an equilateral triangle, taking him into a position from which he can attack or evade. An attack or evasion always incorporates its opposite, simultaneously, as in Wing Chun kung fu (see page 140). It is, the escrimador reasons, no use simply evading an attack, as another will follow. It is better to counter at the same time, to foil any further attacks. There are no fixed, solid stances, as in karate. With knees slightly bent, often balanced on the balls of his feet, the escrimador flows from one point to another, tracing the arabesques of his intricate art. Armed with only one stick, he has one empty hand which is used as a kind of back up. For example, if man A strikes man B, the latter will use his stick to parry the blow, and his back-up empty hand will swiftly guide the armed hand of man A to the side, down or up. Thus freed, man B's weapon hand can attack. This use of the back-up hand is very necessary because such are the intricacies of escrima that a deflected weapon can easily be turned, using the wrist, through another angle to continue the attack. The back-up hand prevents this.

Formal blocking techniques naturally cover the attacking target areas. The block or parry to an attack high up on the body is called a roof block, because the rising back-up hand and the stick make a roof shape. Blocks in escrima are not head-on collisions between one stick and another. If possible the defending stick is sharply angled so that it can slide off into an attack. A knockdown or press-down block is, as its name suggests, an angled pressure to move the attacking stick towards the lower target area, leaving the wrist or upper area free for counterattack. The scabbard block takes place in the position that a sheathed sword would be in, approximately, when held diagonally at a man's side. The gripping hand is nearest the attacker and the stick slopes away to one side. Once the back-up hand has taken the place of the stick, with a swift turn of the wrist a counterattack on the weapon arm of the attacker can take place.

When these and other blocks have been learned, the student can begin friendly informal

Above: *the beginning of a four-part disarming technique, in which the man on the right parries an attack.*

Above: *he attacks in turn and is stopped by a 'roof' block.*

Above left: *his weapon arm is controlled and pressed down.*
Above right: *he is disarmed by means of pressure on the wrist.*

Opposite page: *the fearsome bullwhip is a rarely used escrima weapon, but it can be deadly in the hands of an expert.*

sparring with his partner, using the technical knowledge at his disposal and supplementing it with any combinations that seem natural to him.

For all its linear shape, the escrima stick can become involved in several series of arm entanglements and locks on the body which might prompt the uninitiated to swear that it was made of rubber. These locks are difficult to describe verbally, or even diagrammatically, but the knowledge of their existence can whet one's appetite and indicate that escrima is not just a matter of hitting. Nevertheless, an escrimador would never go into combat with the intention of locking; it would follow from the previous movements. The essence of escrima is not pre-arrangement but instant adaptation to change. Thus a contest might begin with both men out of range, followed by a medium-range then close-range exchange, followed by a close-up lock and 'disarm', the stick being used as a lever to produce pain or pressure. Daniel Inosanto in particular has demonstrated that where the stick goes, the empty hand can go, and vice versa. A stick parry can be a hand parry, the back-up hand can replace the stick or hand parry, the stick thrust can be a punch, and so forth.

Slowly, the student develops into an experienced escrimador and works his way through the labyrinth of techniques. His body will become agile, his arm movements deft and accurate, his field of vision all-embracing. Most strikingly, he will develop a speed of action that he had never thought possible.

From the point of view of self-defence, escrima is excellent training. Although we do not carry sticks, we may carry umbrellas of various lengths, walking sticks, tightly rolled magazines or newspapers which can become improvised weapons of defence. Even without these, the training in body movement and the benefits mentioned above make an admirable preparation for a real-life confrontation.

The psychology of escrima distinguishes it radically from most of the other martial arts. This may partly be due to the fact that it comes from what was, for almost 400 years, a conquered country. Whereas in places such as China and Japan the martial arts were a recognized and accepted part of the culture which could be practised openly and were often encouraged for health and military reasons, in an oppressed country the only martial arts that can exist are those that allow the practitioner to seize the opportunity of the moment, to strike back suddenly with disguised movements involving all the speed and subterfuge that is necessary in guerilla warfare.

PENTJAK SILAT

The archipelago stretching from Malaysia to New Guinea covers a distance of around 5,000 kilometres. It is made up of some three thousand islands and land masses, on which flourish some three thousand styles of pentjak silat for all anyone knows, since there are more than six hundred styles in Malaysia itself and an incalculable number in the rest of the region.

Silat, to use the common abbreviation, is the national fighting art of the archipelago, although for centuries closely guarded Chinese fighting arts coexisted with it. It is an art of weapons use and empty-hand fighting, and has many useful self-defence techniques.

At different periods of its history the archipelago has experienced the peaceful and warlike incursions of Indians, Arabs, Chinese, Portuguese, English, Dutch and Japanese. Although all have left deep cultural marks on the region, the art of silat has remained relatively inviolate, treasured by the people as a heritage which no one could take

from them. Even the contention that in the fourteenth century it was the jealously guarded, sole preserve of the Majapahit sultans is unlikely, given the nature of silat and the vastness of the country. As we will see later, however, while some silat styles may have remained unchanged, researchers such as Donn F. Draeger have found similarities between various techniques and weapons used in the archipelago, and those of other countries.

What is undoubtedly unique to silat, and to Malaysia and Indonesia, is the kris, a wavy-bladed dagger varying in length from 10 to 45 centimetres. Like the samurai sword, its manufacture was regarded at one time as a holy craft, and the methods of production were kept secret. Many people believe that the kris of today is not the true kris, as some of the secrets have been lost. There is some truth in this belief, because the old blades were made from a blend of nickel and the iron from meteorites, and the supply of this type of iron was exhausted around 120 years ago. The blade's

Below left: a technique from silat lincah. The man on the left punches while the defender blocks, raising his leg.
Below right: the defender sweeps his attacker to the ground, with the help of leverage on the arm.

Opposite page: jumping side kick to the head, which contrasts with the many low postures of pentjak silat.

Above left: *the student begins his sequence of movements with the kris, ready to fight.*
Above: *the kris is still in its scabbard, held between thigh and calf.*
Left: *making a straight thrust with the kris, basically a stabbing weapon.*
Below left: *one hand raised in a characteristic position, the other hand and the kris concealed from view.*
Below: *a straight, forward lunge with the kris.*

Above left: *both combatants open up, preparing for and inviting a fight.*
Above right: *the man on the right punches; the defender avoids the punch, delivering a roundhouse kick to the abdomen.*

Below left: *the defender stamps on the back of the attacker's knee, seizes his hair and strikes his neck.*
Below right: *the defender withdraws, raising his leg to avoid a sweeping attack.*

Opposite page, above left: salutation before the fight.
Opposite page, above right, centre and below left: the fight is on, as from a distance the warriors assess one another's style, skill and weakness. They circle one another, getting closer.
Opposite page, below right: at a suitable range they join combat.
Top left: the man on the right punches; the defender drops into the lankah lipat position, grabs the back of the attacker's leg and hits him in the ribs.
Top right: the defender pulls on the attacker's leg, to bring him to the ground.
Centre left: he stamps on the attacker's groin.
Above: the defender steps to the side of the attacker's body, bending his leg and forcing it back towards his head.
Left: the defender reaches forward and pulls on the attacker's neck to increase the pain.

strength came from the many foldings and beatings which the layers of nickel and iron underwent during manufacture.

There are some 40 different types of kris, and over the centuries it has served as a weapon, an object of devotion, an ornament and even as a proxy for a bridegroom marrying a girl of lower caste. It is said that when danger is near, the kris rattles in its sheath, warning its owner. Its presence is thought to bring luck and to ease the pains of childbirth. It is worn in different positions in the sash, for concealment or ease of drawing, and the smaller versions can be hidden by the palm or forearm.

Depending on the spiritual power of the smith, a kris could sometimes perform magic. 'Sorcery by pointing' was one of the examples quoted by Draeger; using a form of sympathetic magic, the owner of a kris could summon up the power of his weapon to penetrate the flesh of an adversary, simply by pointing it in his direction.

As its sword-like nature would suggest, the kris is masculine. Traditionally, every male in the archipelago possessed a kris, and the old laws decreed that a father should present his sons with one at puberty. The unusual wavy blade facilitates the weapon's penetration of the body; it slips through joints and in between bones, and is less difficult to pull out than an ordinary blade. The handle of the kris is at an angle to the blade giving a pistol grip effect, and this assists its use as a thrusting weapon. The sheath, usually made from good quality wood, is called a sarong. Innumerable other bladed weapons exist in Malaysia and Indonesia, but the kris is supreme.

A teacher of silat is called a guru. Robert Smith writes that a teacher was expected to receive no pay 'beyond that necessary to maintain his clothes'. Today there is a more relaxed attitude to this restriction, if it were ever strictly observed. In the past, a prospective student had to prove his worth to the guru, since no men of ill repute were to be admitted to the school. He had to bring with him a chicken, whose blood was spread on the ground as a symbol of the student's blood that might be spilled; a roll of white cloth to be used as a shroud should he die during his training; a knife, as an expression of the alertness or sharpness which he intended to show during his studies; tobacco for the guru to smoke during lulls in training; and money to buy new garments for the guru if they should be torn during practice. Students studied for three hours a night on six days of the week – and training sometimes continued for ten years.

Students of silat need to be fit and supple. They learn how to use the different parts of their

Opposite page, top: opening up the fight in silat lincah stance.
Opposite page, centre: in response to a roundhouse kick, the defender drops into a lankah lipat position.
Opposite page, bottom: the kick is avoided and the defender moves in.
Above left: the defender pulls on the attacker's left leg to bring him down, punches him low in the back and traps his leg with his own leg.
Centre left: the defender continues to pull on the leg so that the attacker is now face down on the floor. He keeps his foot in the attacker's groin.
Below left: the defender jumps over the attacker's body to stamp on his head.

bodies as offensive weapons, and which parts of the body to attack with each 'weapon'. They study posture and footwork, etiquette, sparring, the equivalent of atemi (see page 36), and the use of real weapons. They also receive spiritual training, one of the more verifiable results of which is the ability to restrict the movements of a strong man by holding his wrists 'tenderly', as Robert Smith reports. This ability is akin to that evinced by the most skilled t'ai chi and pakua masters of China.

Silat may take place anywhere – on rocky ground, on soft ground, on wet, slippery ground, even in the sea. The harimau or tiger style of silat is partly designed for fighting in wet mud. As one is sure to slip, it is better to hug the ground like a crouching tiger, and knowledge of how to fight on all fours is necessary since that is where one is likely to find oneself after the first rush. Harimau fighters are skilled in using their feet from this position; they employ kicking, hooking and sweeping movements, launching themselves suddenly forward or back, hands at the ready.

To silat students, the movement of the body and its action in different situations is very important. External behaviour reveals a lot about someone, especially if he is about to fight. What we in the West are re-discovering through the work of behavioural kinesiologists and avant-garde actors and actresses, and repeated contact at a cultural level with people from the East, the Indonesians and Malays already know instinctively. What may look to us like a mere flowery gesture, to a silat man shows, for example, the style of his adversary, his possible intention, his state of mind, or even how fit he is.

Mental concentration, hypnotism, self-hypnotism and suggestion have all been discovered within the various silat systems. These words are,

of course, merely Western symbols for things that none of us understand well, if at all. Their effect on silat masters and students is beyond our comprehension. For example, in 1964 in Djakarta, the capital of Indonesia, a big martial arts demonstration was staged before a large audience which included the late Master Nakayama, a leading figure of the Japan Karate Association. The visiting Japanese karate men showed their powers of breaking wood and after the applause had subsided the Indonesians waited, hoping that someone from the silat camp would show what he could do. Soon a thin, frail-looking Indonesian appeared, carrying a large rock. Master Nakayama and the Japanese karate men examined the rock and declared that it could not be broken by the bare hands of a man. Several other people looked the rock over carefully, to see if there were any cracks in it already. When everyone was satisfied that there was no trickery involved, there was silence for a full five minutes. During this time the frail man concentrated intensely in a way known only to himself. Then, as if in a trance, he reached out for a cup and poured water on his fingers, uttering an incantation. Suddenly, he gave a terrible shout. The boulder crumbled, although the man had not even raised his hand. The audience was awe-struck, looking first at the remains of the rock and then at the man, who was trembling. He continued to tremble for about ten minutes.

In some schools of silat this mysterious energy is gathered from the burial grounds of old masters. A student will be sent to the cemetery to absorb it. Sometimes an object, a talisman, is charged with power; the student keeps the talisman by him and receives power from it. Draeger experienced the healing aspect of silat's invisible energy when he suffered a scalp wound which bled profusely. He was taken to a silat master who placed his hand on the wound; it stopped bleeding immediately and began to heal.

Silat techniques obviously vary widely, but they can conveniently be divided into soft and hard styles. Students of soft styles with flowery movements are told that these are meant to confuse an enemy and give him no chance of assessing when an attack will come. Such movements are impossible to describe in words, and even photographs cannot convey the flowing ease with which they appear to be performed. Many of the recorded styles do, however, have techniques which at times resemble those shown in other sections of this book. The tjikalong style has hand movements similar to those used in Wing Chun, where one hand deflects while the other punches. Although the cross-legged

position of the tjingkrik style is unique to silat, the sudden and explosive rise from the ground can be compared with the ability of the seated Japanese martial artist to rise quickly and go for his opponent. This capacity indicates a strength and suppleness of joint action that is probably only found among nations which habitually sit on the floor. In the setia hatai style a roundhouse kick is used, resembling that of Thai boxing or karate.

A feature of tapak sutji is non-stop movement during combat, and a 360 degree turn of the body about its own axis every few seconds. The nearest Chinese equivalent is probably the non-stop walking of the circle and palm changes of pakua. The training of the senses is found in many martial arts systems, but in setia hati terate silat the eye in particular is trained to observe and estimate the significance of every move the opponent makes. In Japanese and Chinese martial arts, the one-knuckle fist consisting of the folded index or middle finger protruding beyond the others and held firmly by the thumb is a well-known 'weapon', and this is also found in pauh silat. O-soto-gari, the judo technique of sweeping the leg of an opponent from under him, is found in bhakti negara, a modern form of silat, and throws and knife techniques similar to those used in aikido appear in sawi silat. Although these comparisons are valid, they do not detract from the distinctive character of silat.

It should be remembered that the martial arts of Indonesia and Malaysia are generally jutsu rather than 'do' forms, to use Japanese distinctions made clear elsewhere in this book.

The Malaysian style of gayong harimau or tiger was named after a fighter who was known as Allah's Tiger. The techniques are hard and linear, very similar to Japanese karate. Silat pulut, most commonly seen at weddings and ceremonies, is renowned for its beauty and grace. During demonstrations the movements are performed slowly and deliberately. Silat lincah comes from Melaka. Lincah means fast and aggressive, and students of the style attack with lightning speed. Devastating locks applied to the joints are one of its chief characteristics. Silat sendang comes from the Johor region and gets its name from the sideways positioning of the body when confronting an opponent.

Today, silat is widely taught in the West. Competitions are organized so that no fatalities occur, but the fatal techniques are still there in the background. In Japan, for example, the appearance of firearms relegated swordplay as a decisive factor in any battle to an inferior position. In Indonesia and Malaysia, silat continued to be used in tribal warfare alongside the gun, with grim results.

Opposite page, top: in the 'ready' position.
Opposite page, centre: the defender on the left side-steps and deflects a punch.
Opposite page, bottom: the defender strikes the attacker across the chin to twist his head.
Top: the defender continues the turning and twisting movement.
Above: the attacker is brought down, vulnerable to any further counterattack such as a blow to the back.

TAEKWONDO

Opposite page: the power and beauty of taekwondo kicks. They require extraordinary suppleness of the hip joints.

Above: a blocking movement on one leg. This position is characteristic of many 'empty hand' martial arts.
Below: a double blocking position, right arm high and left arm low. Such positions are practised one at a time, and also as part of a form or hyung.

The white-clad figures of taekwondo fighters caught the attention of television audiences across the world during the 1988 Olympics in Korea, the home of this martial art. 'Tae' means to kick or strike with the foot, 'kwon' means to punch or strike with the fist, and 'do' means art. Sometimes called Korean karate, a term which Koreans detest because karate is a Japanese word, taekwondo has two major features which distinguish it from the Japanese martial art: the wide range of kicking techniques and the emphasis on breaking methods.

Perhaps because of their build or innate physical ability, the Koreans can kick with extraordinary ease. They are also exceptionally tough and this is reflected in the taekwondo grading syllabus: all students must learn how to smash bricks, wood and tiles with their bare hands and feet for the 'destruction' tests. Taekwondo forms part of the training of every Korean soldier. The Tiger battalions of Korea fighting in Vietnam were said to have had the clearest sectors of all the units involved. The Vietcong stayed out of their way, recognizing what they were up against.

Some 1,400 years ago a martial art existed in Korea called t'aekyon, and it is maintained that this was the precursor of taekwondo. Ancient Korea was divided into three kingdoms: Silla, Baekchae and Koguryo. Silla was the smallest of the three and always feared being overrun by the much larger Koguryo kingdom. During the sixth century AD the King of Silla, Chin-Hung, took steps to provide a more adequate defence force and organized a military group of strong young men called the hwarang-do. Regular physical and moral discipline forged this group into a formidable fighting force and part of their training was in t'aekyon. According to modern authorities, t'aekyon styles did not change very much until the Japanese occupation. From 1910 onwards Chinese and Japanese empty-hand techniques were introduced, transforming the old art into what it is today, although since 1955 other modifications have been made.

After the liberation of Korea in 1945, a search began for a new word to replace t'aekyon. It took ten years for agreement to be reached, but finally the new name of taekwondo was accepted, having

Top to bottom: both students take up typical sparring postures. Next, the man tries a reverse punch which the woman blocks. Then the woman continues to turn to her right, preparing for a kick. Finally, she jumps up and at the same time delivers a kick under her partner's armpit.

Opposite page: demonstrating simultaneous high kicks.

Above: the woman produces a devastating high back kick, lifting her partner off the floor.
Below: as the man tries a round kick to the face, the woman beats him to it with a high front kick.

Opposite page: as the woman tries a high round kick, the man drops to the floor to strike low and knock her off balance.

been submitted by Choi Hong Hi. This military man was one of the strongest postwar supporters and promulgators of taekwondo, and under his guidance it was demonstrated to armed forces all over the world as a toughening-up system. The administrative side of any martial arts organization is often as tough and combative as the art it represents and taekwondo did not escape from this. As a result of internal politics, it is not internationally unified, although technical differences between individual groups are insignificant.

The empty-hand techniques of the Korean system are very similar to those of Japanese karate (see page 6). The same may be said of its blocks and stances, although one notable block, the W-shape or san makki, is peculiar to taekwondo. To perform this block both arms are raised, bent at the elbow to form a W shape; the fingertips and head make up the three points, while the arms and neck form the body of the letter.

When one looks at kicking techniques, things are different. The original Okinawan type of karate which was taken to Japan in the 1920s had few kicks during Gichin Funakoshi's time (see page 8). Later, the roundhouse kick was introduced, but even when karate arrived in Europe during the 1960s the syllabus did not include as many kicks as are now taught. In that department taekwondo was ahead, and still is. It has all manner of kicks delivered in midair, requiring powerful springing action, acrobatic control of the whole body in flight, and the ability to focus a powerful blow while still up there!

Critics, many of them perhaps envious, say such things as 'You cannot do a flying kick in a telephone box', ignoring the obvious fact that if attacked in a telephone box a taekwondo student would use his fist or knee like anyone else. What these critics do not understand is the relationship between a martial art and its place of origin. Korea

Above: *a flying side kick to the head is common in taekwondo competitions.*
Below: *a double jumping front kick blocked by a double blocking technique.*

Opposite page: *a jumping stamping kick, showing characteristic agility.*

has large areas of open country, where people use horses, so it is feasible that an unarmed man might find it useful to be able to leap high and kick someone off a horse or pony. Another technical criticism of high kicks is that while in midair a man cannot orientate himself and is therefore vulnerable to attack from the ground. In fact this depends on the particular situation, but even in unfavourable conditions an advanced taekwondo student's ability to govern his airborne activity is highly developed. One can only imagine that those who voice this particular criticism are lacking in sufficient experience of the art.

Taekwondo students wear uniforms similar to those used for karate, although in recent years a new type of uniform has emerged in the shape of a slipover top, of the same cut and length as the old wrapover jacket but more convenient. The tallyon chu, the equivalent of the Japanese makiwara, is a long post set in the ground with straw bound round the top and lower parts for kicking and punching practice. The tallyon kune, now often replaced by a modern apparatus, consists of a straw-bound log suspended by ropes at each end, which hold it at adjustable distances from the ground. This is also used for kicking and punching, but is particularly instrumental in developing the leaping tactics of the art. A student leaps over the log and while in flight directs a kick at it.

During the late 1970s and the 1980s what can almost be called a craze developed. It was centred around the word 'stretching'. Top taekwondo and karate men all over the world began to foster the notion that it was essential to be able to do the splits to facilitate high kicks. Stretching was on everyone's lips and different pieces of apparatus emerged, varying from a simple rope attached to an overhead beam, which could be used to pull one leg up while keeping the other on the floor, to an expensive 'stretch machine'. At the same time a number of

Wearing body armour, the students shown on this page and opposite can make full contact without fear of serious injury.

stands which could support wood or tiles were introduced for training in the destruction techniques.

In taekwondo, the patterns of movement that are equivalent to the kata performed by karate students are called 'hyung'. According to Choi Hong Hi there are three schools of hyung: Sorim, Soryong and Ch'ang-Hon. The hyung they exhibit were devised by different taekwondo masters at different times. Although some groups in various parts of the world have modified the traditional hyung, the basic idea of doing them to train in all the movements and combinations of the art remains the same. One of the traditional hyung is called hwa-rang, after the early youthful protectors of Silla. Yul-kok is named after the 'Confucius of Korea', Yi I (AD 1536–84). Tong-il celebrates the unification of ancient Korea into one nation. Most unusually, and probably uniquely among Eastern martial arts, nearly all the hyung of the Ch'ang-Hon school bear the names of famous men. In a sense, therefore, a journey through the hyung of this school is a journey through history.

Regrettably, on a personal level there is no love lost between Japanese and Korean martial artists, however much they may respect one another's native martial arts. Add to this the dissimilarities between karate and taekwondo, and it is not surprising that there has been no merging between the two. If in future taekwondo is to remain part of the Olympics, then more ructions lie in wait for the movement if karate organizations find themselves excluded. Although this forms no part of a beginner's considerations when he is setting out on the long martial arts trail, it may help him to understand some of the undercurrents in any club or association which he may join.

Competition in taekwondo is fierce. In the 1970s Jhoon Rhee, the Korean who is popularly known as the father of American taekwondo, invented his famous Safe-T sparring equipment which, together with body armour, was used in its latest form at the 1988 Olympics. Many others have copied his designs, but he was undoubtedly the originator. The no-contact rule mentioned in the section on kick boxing (see page 180) dogged all the martial arts, but the introduction of padded gloves, boots, body armour and headguards enabled people to fight without getting seriously hurt, although in the Olympics at least one bad kick on the groin found its way onto the screen. As in karate, once Westerners had studied taekwondo for a sufficient period of time, they began to sweep the board in competitions, in a manner that Koreans had at one time thought impossible. The myth that oriental people would always be the best at their native arts began to disintegrate when

Above: the taekwondo version of a focus mitt, held high for accuracy training.
Below: the focus mitt held slightly lower, again for accuracy in kicking.

Opposite page: training with a special flexible pad, as a preliminary to breaking wooden boards.

a Dutchman, Anton Geesink – admittedly a giant – defeated all-comers in judo after World War II, and there must have been much grief in the hearts of the Japanese when their top karate team was defeated by Europeans in the 1970s.

There are several other Korean martial arts including hwarang-do, hapkido, tang soo do and kuk sool. Hwarang-do illustrates the desire of all Eastern martial artists to be associated with illustrious figures from the past. Just as Chinese kung fu students like to associate their art with Bodhidharma, however remote this association may be, so Korean martial artists like to be associated with the kingdom of Silla and the young men of the hwarang-do. Hapkido is very much a synthesis of other systems and its syllabus, which includes the use of judo and karate techniques in profusion as well as self-defence and high-kicking methods, points to a modern conception. Similarly, the other arts listed above also consist of a variety of throwing, kicking, punching and grappling techniques, although each has a particular emphasis. The arresting forms of hapkido have been adopted by several police forces in the United States and the more secret techniques of hwarang-do have been whispered to be part of the fighting repertoire of various official covert operations groups around the world. The same distinction has been claimed by at least one taek-

wondo expert. When Ki Jeong Lee emigrated to the United States in 1982 and established his own school, magazine headlines announced that 'his masterful skills have taken him from South America where he taught CIA agents . . .', and many people must have thought that this referred to the Central Intelligence Agency. Further reading revealed that it was the Colombian Intelligence Agency – no doubt just as efficient but hardly the same.

Less widely known Korean arts include sul sa, the equivalent of Japanese ninjutsu (see page 70), and po bok sul which involves rope-tying techniques. Probably as a result of Mongolian influences, the favoured weapon of ancient Korea was the bow and arrow. Genghis Khan, the conqueror of much of Asia, used mounted archers with irresistible effect. Centuries later, reports indicate that the silent bow was used in the Korean War of the 1950s. Korea even has its own version of a wrestling art similar to sumo (see page 78), and once again authorities point to Mongolian sources, wrestling being a favourite sport among those peoples. The name of this art is cireum, which is similar to the Mongolian word for wrestling, 'cilnem'.

The question of grading and gaining a higher rank in the echelons of taekwondo, or any other Korean martial art, is one which faces the beginner and continues throughout his martial arts career.

The origin of the coloured belts worn by the various grades seems to be lost as far as historical verification is concerned, but one theory states that they are based on the different coloured banners carried by Chinese armies. Whatever the truth of its beginnings, it is a sad fact that today the grading system has mainly become a question of technical skill, while the simultaneous refining of the character is ignored. There are oases of exceptions to this generalization, however, and one of these is Ken Cheung. In an article in *Taekwondo Times* magazine, in May 1987, he described the inner significance of the coloured belt system and his admirable explanation is outlined here.

The white belt of the beginner denotes purity or innocence. It shows that a beginner, in his understandable ignorance, should be open-minded, showing trust in the art and the teacher. The yellow belt stands for gold or truth, and also for seed which can grow. An ancient saying states that in order to make gold one must first possess a small quantity of it. The gold and the seed signify that the student, in attaining his yellow belt, is laying the foundations of future development. As one might expect, the colour green symbolizes growth, aliveness and change. A student who has reached the green belt grade should look for those things in himself. Attainments in one competition should not hold one back from further growth; one should not rest on one's laurels. The blue belt represents the sky. Just as there is no end to the sky's depth, so a more mature student realizes that he cannot see the depth of his chosen art, his chosen path. This enables him to face difficulties, knowing that in overcoming them he will mature even further. The red belt, not to be confused with the beginner's red belt worn in some judo schools, stands for the sun. In human terms this is the energy and determination which the student brings to his studies.

When Taekwondo Strikes is the name of a famous martial arts film which now has the status of a cult movie. But the most recent and continuously popular films are *Karate Kid*, parts one and two. Karate buffs may be surprised to discover that it was a taekwondo expert, Pat Johnson, who did much of the coaching for these minor epics. This incongruity between the name of a movie and the art used in it shows that the film world is a law unto itself and gives a hint to the martial arts world about what course it should follow.

From a standing position the student goes into a 'splits' position as he smashes a heap of tiles, using the thumb edge of his hand.

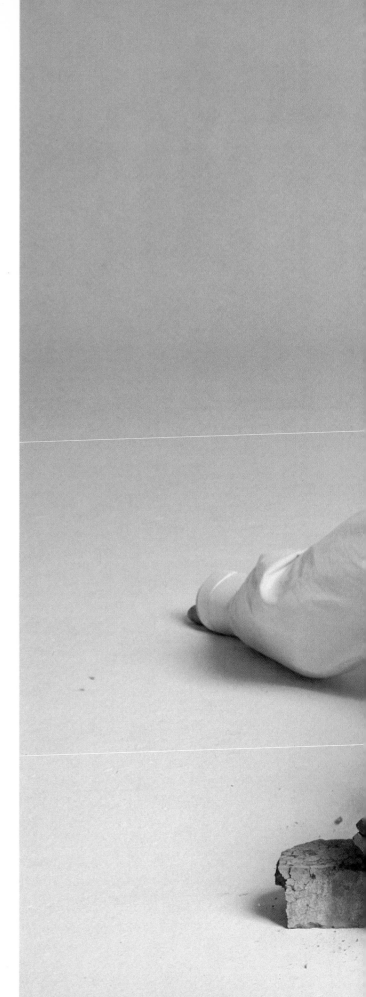

KICK BOXING

Boxing and kick boxing are cousins. While one is purely Western, with the Queensberry rules firmly behind it, the other is an amalgam of techniques from several martial arts, including boxing itself. The atmosphere, the cries of the crowd, the ring, the seconds, the referee and judges, the time keeper, the knockouts, the protests and the money are all part of both scenes.

To understand how kick boxing came about, it is necessary to go back about 25 years. In the early 1960s America's first martial arts magazines, which usually showed photographs of judo exponents in their heavy unbleached cotton outfits, began to feature men in white, stylishly cut suits. These men were kicking, punching, blocking and shouting as they moved. They were doing kara-te, literally empty-hand fighting, a type of unarmed combat picked up by a group of GIs during a tour of duty in Japan. The martial arts world, primarily concerned with judo, aikido and kendo, took little notice at first. But soon karate began to spread. Japanese sensei (instructors) took up residence in the United States and Europe. Students began to flock to their dojos and by the mid-60s karate was taking off.

Karate, originally meant to be used to kill the enemy with one blow, was only allowed to develop in the States and Europe as a 'no contact' sport. Participants were awarded a point for an accurately delivered near miss. Although sport karate grew in popularity, many people found that this way of winning was unsatisfactory. In judo you threw your man or held him down for a specified time. In boxing you knocked him to the ground. In wrestling you pinned his shoulders. But in karate you scored without touching your opponent.

Slowly, some students of karate and boxing began to experiment. A teacher of Korean karate, Jhoon Rhee, brought out his own fist and foot protectors, and began to stage 'full contact' bouts of a new style of fighting using the hands and feet. It drew large crowds; professional kick boxing had arrived.

At first, this new form was known simply as 'full contact'. Fighters such as Joe Lewis and Chuck Norris, later to star in many martial arts films, appeared on the scene. They were well muscled,

In this purposely contrived photograph a breakdown of the sequence of actions used to perform a flying side kick is shown. Notice how the attacker gathers his legs up before launching his kick, and keeps his hands in an on guard position throughout. His opponent raises his hands in a characteristic blocking position, to protect his head and face.

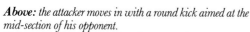

Above: *the attacker moves in with a round kick aimed at the mid-section of his opponent.*
Below: *this front kick is driven forward and up to the head. It can equally well be used to attack the body or legs.*

tough, athletic. Then came Bill 'Superfoot' Wallace, a fighter who could flick out his feet like a fly catcher's tongue; his kick was as fast as a punch. Later still the Canadian ace, Jean Yves Theriault, shot to stardom and reputedly signed a million-dollar advertising contract.

Meanwhile, in Thailand, the centuries-old art of Thai boxing continued to flourish. This art, using gloves but no padding on the feet, is a national sport, and has a close relationship with modern kick boxing. Thai boxing instructors began to descend on Europe to impart their knowledge. At the same time Japanese fight promoters saw a promising source of income in the new fist and foot contests, and soon film and video makers

jumped on the bandwagon, sensing that here was an opportunity to make big money.

So what is kick boxing? Although it is an amalgam, it has its own individual style. The kicks that are used are mainly roundhouse and front kicks, reverse roundhouse kicks, spinning back kicks and stamping kicks, all of which are described elsewhere in this book. Karate, taekwondo, kung fu and boxing have all contributed to kick boxing. The punches that are used come mainly from boxing, as do the blocks. The rules are a little more complicated in that in every kick boxing round a certain number of kicking attacks have to be used and a judge must keep track of them. This is to ensure that the bout does not develop into an ordinary boxing contest. It is a fact that most of the damage in kick boxing is done by punches. Bouts are usually shorter than boxing bouts, since the demands on the kick fighters are greater. It requires much more energy to kick than it does to punch. The participants wear gloves and padded boots with no soles.

Kick boxing may be taught in kung fu, Thai boxing and karate clubs, but if you join a club that specializes in kick boxing you should be prepared for a hard time. Rough and tough are the order of the day. You will be expected to undergo all the training associated with ordinary boxing, plus much that has been imported from Thailand and Japan. You can expect to be hit during training and only if you can sustain this should you consider joining a club. Not surprisingly, a doctor's certificate of fitness is nearly always required.

Training can be divided into two main sections. Stamina and fitness sessions include jogging, building up the body to take punishment, skipping and weight training. Preparation for fighting includes bag work, hook and jab pad work, technique training and sparring with a partner. There are all kinds of more exotic training aids which the interest in the art has summoned forth from the minds of sports equipment manufacturers, and these serve to stimulate interest in continuing training and reaching higher levels of performance.

Kick boxing appeals to many different types of people; its devotees are not solely mindless, inarticulate young men. Many karate students drift towards kick boxing because they want to see whether or not they can really fight. The top fighters earn big money, especially in the United States, so this, and the accompanying prestige and sense of achievement, is an added incentive, particularly in times of economic uncertainty.

Unlike most of the martial arts under consideration in this book, there is no discernible philosophy in kick boxing; the idea is to win. This is also true of Western and Thai boxing. In kick boxing the reason may lie both in its varied origins and in the way it developed. Although some individual fighters are reputed to have specific attitudes to fighting and certain little-known physical and psychological training methods, there is no general background of thought, no charming historical anecdotes, no old sayings – just punches, kicks and sweat.

Thai boxing

In Thailand there are over 100,000 boxers, ranging from village hopefuls to top-class professionals. In other countries, although Thai boxing is popular and clubs hold their own contests, students of the art often compete in tournaments organized by kick boxing clubs, which have a far greater number of members.

Thai boxing is technically very similar to kick boxing and is also not unlike savate (see page 186). However, grappling in a standing position plays a much bigger part in Thai boxing than in any other hitting style. A favourite on-guard position in the ring involves holding both fists at the same height on either side of the head. This gives protection against roundhouse kicks. The shin is used both as a striking and defending part of the body, and one of the favourite methods of weakening an opponent is to strike him on vulnerable parts of the leg or upper arm, using the shin bone. Elbows and knees are used at close quarters to inflict telling damage. Thai boxing is a tough sport and preparation for contests is gruelling.

Much of the equipment associated with Western boxing is used in training. For example, students work with big punching and kicking bags and small target pads held in the hand of a partner. Skipping, and bunny hops in a squatting position, also help to build up fitness and stamina. For the actual contests, fighters wear wide-legged shorts and boxing gloves, and bandage their ankles and insteps. There are five three-minute rounds per contest, with two-minute breaks between rounds. Because Thai boxing is so much more demanding than ordinary boxing, longer bouts would use up too much energy and inflict too much punishment on the contestants. A small orchestra of drums, cymbals and flutes heralds each contest and 'serenades' the fighters during rounds, in an effort to spur them on to greater endeavours. Combined with the roars of the crowd this music produces pandemonium. When the contestants enter the ring they bow to the crowd and their trainers, then perform a series of ritual movements to banish fear from their hearts.

Rather like the junior sumotori (see page 78), the young Thais who wish to make a career of the fight game join a particular school or 'camp', where they learn the techniques and rituals associated with the school. When a fighter begins to take part in real tournaments, he wears a mongkon or thin cord around his head. The mongkon is part of the national costume; it is worn during the pre-fight ritual, then removed for the fighting.

In Thailand, a boxer's life is tough and not very rewarding financially unless he becomes one of the top ten fighters. Often the students adopt nicknames such as green dragon or tiger, to show that they have the fighting characteristics of the creature concerned.

Outside Thailand the opportunities to make money as a fighter vary. In Britain the rewards are small, but should a fighter manage to join a kick boxing circuit in North America the financial prospects can be good. However, not many Westerners are prepared to commit themselves to the strenuous and prolonged training that is required in Thailand.

Japanese promoters and fighters do not like to refer to kick boxing as Thai boxing. In the 1970s there was a great deal of bad blood between Japanese kick boxing and Thai boxing fraternities. Because the Thais have for centuries been proud of their native fighters, it was a matter of grave concern to them when one of their men was defeated by a Japanese. In this controversial fight the Thai contestant was knocked out when his Japanese opponent fell down on top of him, causing his head to strike the floor very hard indeed. The Japanese fighter was not disqualified, although many thought that he should have been, and in the Thai camps there was consternation and uproar.

A similar incident occurred in connection with Thai boxing and kung fu. A few years before the Japanese versus Thai bout, a team of kung fu fighters from Hong Kong went to Thailand and were thrashed by native martial artists. Chinese martial arts magazines hurried to defend their compatriots, claiming that the kung fu men were amateurs whereas the Thai boxers were professional, and dreaming up as many excuses as possible. Nevertheless, the verdicts stood and the Chinese in Hong Kong have been smarting ever since. Just as the magic spells used in the Boxer Rebellion did not save the Boxers from Western bullets, so the 'chi' of the kung fu men did not protect them from the kicks of the Thai boxers. The whole thing really boiled down to toughness and fighting expertise.

Thai boxing made its debut more than a thousand years ago. As the hordes of Genghis Khan flooded into northern China, many inhabitants left in haste and some went to Thailand (Siam). One theory states that much of Thai boxing came from the influence of Chinese martial arts on the indigenous fighting methods. Another upholds the notion that the frequent disputes between Thailand, Burma and Vietnam were instrumental in producing many developments in both armed and unarmed combat, and that Thai boxing was part of this process.

Legend has it that a famous Thai boxer who had been captured by the Burmese was granted his freedom after beating no fewer than 12 Burmese fighters. A tournament is held annually in his memory. During the fourteenth century, the debate concerning the Thai succession was settled by a boxing bout. Fang Keng and Ji Kumkam were the only sons of the deceased king, Sen Muang Mu. Rather than plunge the country into civil war, the two young men agreed to fight each other, not personally but through two surrogate champions. Ji Kumkam's man won and he became king. Possibly the most famous story about Thai boxing comes from a sixteenth-century manuscript. It concerns a fight between the Thai prince, Narusen, also called the Black Prince, and the son of Bayinnaung, King of Burma. The fight lasted for hours, but in the end the Black Prince killed the king's son. The Burmese had been about to invade Thailand, but as a result of the contest they decided against it.

Burmese bando
Until recently very little information came out of Burma, so it is no surprise that its favourite martial art, bando, has not been exported to the West. Bando means the way of defence, and may have come from Tibet via China. Like Thai boxing it is more than a thousand years old.

Specialists may not accept the contention that bando is similar to kick boxing and Thai boxing, but for the most part it is. A single major difference is that unlike the other styles choking techniques are allowed. Aficionados of bando also claim that it is a tougher fighting art. Certainly the contestants do not wear gloves but only bandage their fists.

After World War II, when Burma became independent, the International Bando Association was founded in Rangoon, in honour of those who had died in the war in Asia. At once it began to reinstate the art that had been officially banned by the British since 1885.

Although bando is rarely practised outside Burma, in the United States there is a bando association which does not advertise itself and remains staunchly non-profit-making. Its symbol is the black panther, and its uniform is black, to remind members of those who died in the war and that every day one faces the unknown.

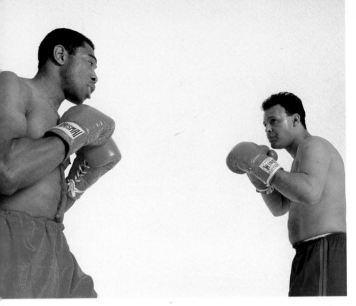

Punching techniques play a bigger part in kick boxing than kicking techniques. This is partly explained by the greater ease of throwing a punch and by the fact that once a kick attack has been made both fighters tend to move into closer range. Close-range kicking is seen but is the exception rather than the rule.

Above left: the man on the right is moving in and is considering a right cross punch.
Above right: as his opponent sends out a left jab it is palmed down.
Below: continuing his attack, the man on the right grabs his opponent's outstretched left arm and scores with a heavy right to the jaw. Unlike orthodox Western boxing it is permitted in kick boxing to grab, hold and even throw down an opponent, in addition to kicking him. In some contests where an equal number of points has been scored and a decision is needed, the winner is the man who has displayed the widest variety of techniques.

SAVATE

Savate, or *boxe Française*, has some of the elegance of a Paris salon, the toughness of an old sea dog, and the technical quality found in the best amateur boxing. Many good karate students have taken up savate, then returned with haste to the dojo, nursing their injuries and grateful to be back in the safety of the no-contact fold. Savate demands courage, fitness and the kind of stiff upper lip so often associated with the Englishman when his back is to the wall. But in this case the style of combat is French, through and through.

Savate contests take place in a boxing ring. The contestants wear gloves similar to boxing gloves but with longer cuffs. Present-day costume consists of a leotard, for complete freedom of movement, and specially constructed shoes with aston-

ishingly hard toecaps. A kick from one of these shoes can break a rib, crack an arm and stun the brain.

Although the techniques used in savate are superficially similar to those of boxing and karate, on closer examination many of them can be seen to be different. For example, the *chassé* kick is like a side kick in karate, a thrusting type of kick, but often when it is delivered the arm furthest away from the kicking leg is raised, to balance the leg, after the fashion of a classic French swordsman using a rapier. Another unusual feature of savate is the use of an upright, cross-legged position, either as

Above: *as the man on the left delivers* a coup de pied bas, *his opponent leaps up with a high kick to the face.*
Opposite page, left: *a high* chassé *kick to the face balanced by the high rear arm.*
Opposite page, right: *a scoring* coup de pied bas *to the lower leg.*

a preparation for turning, or as a means of moving forwards or backwards. This type of technique is frowned on in karate and boxing.

In the *chassé* which resembles a side kick the hips are turned, but there is another kind of *chassé* which is similar to a front kick in karate, except that instead of being a flicking, hinged kick, it also employs a thrusting movement. The *fouetté* is a kicking technique in which the leg is brought round in a curve and at the last minute the lower leg is whipped into action using the toe to strike the opponent. *Fouettés* must be horizontally applied.

Like the *chassé* and the *fouetté*, the *coup de pied bas* or low kick illustrates the emphasis on balance in savate. As its name suggests, the *coup* is delivered below the knee of an opponent either to knock him off balance, injure him or prevent him from kicking. When performing this technique the attacker leans back, so there is a straight line between his shoulders and the striking foot. In addition there are three reverse kicks or *revers*. One of these, the *revers frontal*, is similar to the karate crescent kick; the kicking leg sweeps in front of the supporting leg, then goes back across and up to the opponent's head.

Punches are made up of jabs, crosses, hooks, swings and uppercuts, very similar to those of boxing. Although the swings, mainly delivered with the

rear fist, appear to be telegraphed, they often strike the target. This may be because savate fighters have not just the fists to watch out for, but the feet too!

Defending techniques consist of blocks or *parades* and evasions or *esquives*. These are used in combination, and will be followed by a counter-attack or *riposte*. Once a student knows the basic techniques, he can go on to learn the combinations or *enchaînements*. An opponent may launch a series of punches and kicks from different angles and the defender must know how to put his defence together to cope with them all, looking out for a chance to hit back. Unless his opponent is 'like a blacksnake after a couple of rabbits', to quote from Joseph Moncure's epic boxing poem *The Set-Up*, he will find this opportunity, using the combinations or *enchaînements* he has learned. Among the evasive tactics is the *déplacement*, a kind of side step which can be a preparatory movement for a counterpunch or counterkick.

Photographs of savate contestants do not have the oriental flavour or the mysterious dynamism of those of karate students, but it would be a mistake to underestimate the danger of an encounter with a seasoned savate exponent. Interestingly, just like judo-ka, students of savate follow a grading system based on knowledge and proficiency.

Right: *the attacker on the left prepares to perform a kicking technique.*
Below left: *the attacker is trying to mislead the defender into thinking that the kick is coming from the defender's right side, to the low or middle region of his body.*
Below right: *instead, he attacks with a high fouetté kick to the left side of the face.*
Opposite page, left: *the attacker draws back his right fist as the defender covers up.*
Opposite page, right: *he delivers a right hooking punch to the face. The clear 'signal' that he gives, by drawing back the fist in a very obvious way, does not prevent this type of punch from getting through. He might be about to kick with either leg, or launch a jab with his left fist, so the defender can never be sure of what is coming.*

Colours, relating to the gloves rather than the belt, indicate the particular grade. The order is blue, green, red, white and yellow. The holder of a *gant jaune* or yellow glove, the highest non-competitive grade, can go on to compete for the *gant de bronze*. The final grades are three levels of *gant d'argent* or silver glove.

The main controlling body for savate is the *Fédération Française de Boxe Française-Savate et Disciplines Assimilées*. Outside France, savate has slowly but surely grown in popularity, and many of the world's leading martial artists have expressed an interest in it. However, it is unlikely that it will become affiliated with any of the oriental martial arts. One reason for this is the difference in permitted techniques, as well as the difference in attire.

At the end of the eighteenth century, savate was making a name for itself in the waterfront bars of southern France. In seaports such as Marseilles, sailors demonstrated their skill in footfighting in no uncertain manner. It is said that they picked up their new methods during voyages to Eastern countries. An old French print shows a group of sailors on board ship watching a savate contest, with one of the fighters resting his hand on the deck to support a high kick.

Other people wanted to learn this new fighting method, and in 1820 Michel Casseux (known in the quarter where he lived as Pisseux) opened his first gym or *salle* in Paris. Savate appealed to the upper classes; the Duke of Orléans and the artist Gavarni are both known to have taken lessons. At that time some kind of slapping technique was used instead of punching and it was only later that a pupil of Casseux, Charles Lecour, introduced closed-fist punches. This occurred after he was beaten by an English boxer called Owen Swift. However, it is reported that the famous bare-knuckle fighter John L. Sullivan was given a very hard time by a savate expert. Lecour studied boxing in London, then opened his own *salle* in Paris in 1830.

Mugging, nineteenth-century style, was a problem in France and many people learned savate to protect themselves in the street. Allied to the empty-hand style was the method called *la canne d'arme* or fighting with a cane. This highly dangerous and effective art involved thrusting and 'whipping', using the cane at high speed to rupture blood vessels and cause other serious injuries. Savate was not welcomed by the authorities, but it spread nevertheless.

Among the famous characters of the savate

world was Louis Vigneron, 'the cannon man', who defeated Dickson, an English boxer, but later spent time in prison for accidentally throwing a friend out of a second storey window and killing him. The cannon was a real one weighing 305 kilos, which Vigneron supported on his shoulder. When it was fired, one of his pupils called Alexandrini would catch the cannonball. This demonstration of strength eventually cost both men their lives.

The man who really put savate on the map was Joseph Charlemont. Born in France in 1839, he taught the art to recruits until war broke out with Prussia in 1870. When France lost, he fled to Belgium because of the subsequent political unrest, and set up another *salle* in Brussels. He introduced a set of rules that compare in importance with those drawn up by the Marquess of Queensberry for English boxing. In 1878 Charlemont was able to return to his native country, where he carried on teaching, attracting such notables as the writer Alexandre Dumas. At the time of Queen Victoria's golden jubilee he visited England and fought exhibition bouts with such effect that he was praised in the famous magazine *The Sporting Life*, which referred to him as one of the 'Paris kickers'.

In the first decade of this century the world-famous French boxer Georges Carpentier was an avid savate student, but later he devoted himself to English boxing where his coolness and often gentlemanly behaviour in the ring won him wide acclaim.

The rounds in savate are shorter than boxing rounds; they last for one minute, one and a half minutes or two minutes, with a one-minute break between rounds. The only protection worn is a gumshield and groin protector. There is a referee who ensures fair play and sees that all the simple etiquette relating to the spectators, the seconds and the fighters is observed. Points are scored and a knockout or severe injury signals the end of the contest. If the fight goes the distance, whichever contestant has scored the most points is the winner. An important aspect of scoring is that kicking techniques must outnumber punching techniques.

Opposite page, above left: *a series of punching exchanges begins with a low uppercut to the abdomen, delivered by the man on the right.*
Opposite page, above right: *the uppercut is blocked and the defender on the left replies with a right cross punch.*
Opposite page, below: *a series of counter punches follows, typical of an actual contest or free-sparring session.*
Right: *a demonstration of a typical uppercut rising to the chin.*

This rule, similar to one employed in kick boxing (see page 180), ensures that the fight does not develop into a boxing match. The awarding of points matches this idea: one for a punch, one for a low kick, two for a medium-high kick and three for a high kick. A knockout is the same as in boxing, requiring a count of ten, and as in amateur boxing three knockdowns in one round signal the end of the contest.

Training, apart from going through the techniques of the art, consists of running and skipping, stretching, press-ups using the knuckles and light work-outs with weights. Students also study the use of the cane, to speed up their reflexes. Like all athletes, savate fighters must learn to pace themselves and not use up all their energy in one or two rounds. Shadow boxing helps to develop this ability and students try to spread their strength equally through six rounds or more.

Although savate attacks are powerful, the contests themselves are fast moving and a student must learn to move about rapidly, never stopping, so that he will provide his opponent with a difficult target. Such tactics found their way gradually into sport karate (see page 6) also and one often sees karate fighters bouncing up and down on both feet during a bout.

In boxing, fighters are regularly seen tapping an opponent's gloves, and wasting a lot of energy

Above: *the attacker raises his left foot in preparation for a kicking attack.*
Above right: *the attacker delivers a descending heel kick.*
Centre left: *squaring up for a sparring session.*
Centre right: *the attacker on the left turns away in preparation for a kick.*

Bottom left: *the attacker completes his turn, ready for a revers or reverse kick.*
Bottom right: *he launches a high revers which the defender blocks.*
Opposite page: *a sequence of free-sparring movements in which kicks and punches are exchanged.*

with these unproductive actions. In *Savate – Boxe Française*, one of the few books on the subject in English, authors Reed and Muggeridge say: 'Hit him as hard as you can to make him worry.' To this end, students train to hit hard every time, leaving the tapping to the boxers.

In Japanese martial arts, non-Japanese students must learn the terminology of their art in its original language. In savate, the terms used are all in French. One advantage of this is that everyone all over the world speaks the same language – a big contribution to common understanding of what is taking place.

Like kick boxing, savate today has little in the way of tradition. It has no religious connections, no legends, and no theme of self-development running through it. It is an art involving hard work, hard fighting and, if you manage it, the glory of winning.

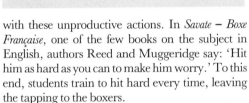

HYBRIDS

Since the late 1960s a number of highly derivative martial arts have established themselves, or are in the process of doing so. The reasons why such arts have been developed are interesting and perhaps shed light on those older martial arts whose histories have only scanty evidence and conjecture to support them.

'Nunchaku combat' derives from Ryukyu kobujutsu (see page 62). Inspired by Bruce Lee to train in the use of this weapon, many martial arts students were disappointed to discover that it was too dangerous to be used in competitions. To overcome this limitation, a softer type of nunchaku was developed in the 1980s which could strike a person without causing damage. A newly designed headguard, plus existing Wing Chun or taekwondo body armour, insured against mishaps during tournaments, and largely under French influence the new nunchaku combat system appeared. A scoring method was introduced and several international tournaments have taken place. Training is geared towards scoring points, and therefore differs greatly from traditional methods. An exciting and exhilarating sport, it has few of the 'do' or jutsu elements, but appeals to those who do not want to go through the rigours of standard nunchaku training.

During the 1950s judo was much more popular than it is today. Occasionally, articles were published on a Russian martial art called sambo, which is similar to judo but includes elements of wrestling. The participants wear short trunks and a judo-style jacket. The art dates from about 1938 when Russia's regional wrestling styles, plus some techniques that obviously derived from judo, were synthesized and given an umbrella title. Although around 50 years old, sambo has only become well known as the martial arts in general have flourished. There are now associations all over the world and women participate as well as men. It is standard training for Russian soldiers and police.

In the United States the 'gun lobby' regularly refer to a citizen's right to bear arms, when arguing their case. The tradition of possessing firearms obviously goes back to the days of the early settlers when a weapon was a necessity. Whether or not

this tradition should be perpetuated is outside the scope of this book, but the fact remains that interest in guns is strong in North America, and any fighting method ancillary to gun use has always found favour. At the beginning of this century President Theodore Roosevelt gave impetus to this outlook. When Roosevelt was studying at Harvard university, one of his fellow students, a Japanese nobleman by the name of Keneko Kentaro, had arranged for him to have jujutsu lessons. In addition, Roosevelt was a boxer, an explorer and a revolver and rifle expert. In contrast to these bellicose attributes, he later won the Nobel peace prize. Other figures and events in modern American history, especially the Vietnam War and the threat of Communism, have fed the flames of this image of a home-grown 'Yankee samurai'.

After returning from Vietnam, some of the veterans set up schools teaching gun use, self-defence and survival methods, responding to the public's fears of growing violence and the possible after-effects of a nuclear war, as well as satisfying the desire of many young men to turn themselves into latter-day samurai warriors. Such schools range from those aimed at showing ordinary people how to deal with intruders, muggers and rapists, to those that set out to train mercenaries. The term to describe this type of training is the New Breed system. Interest in the system has been greatly stimulated by the Rambo films.

The authorities have kept a watchful and at times nervous eye on this phenomenon all over the Western world, and unfortunately for those traditional martial arts whose methods are contiguous to it, the authorities have been keeping an unnecessarily nervous eye on them also. One may justifiably say that as hybridization or genetic experimentation may have its dangers for the orthodox stock, so a similar phenomenon in the martial arts world has its pitfalls.

Kaju-kenbo is a much more middle of the road and sound hybrid. This was the brainchild of Adriano Emperado of Hawaii, who saw a growing need for a modern martial arts system which bypassed much that is traditional and focused on the current need for self-defence, particularly on the street. Emperado was a student of two famous teachers, William Chow and James Mitose. With

Opposite page, above: a sideways scoring strike used in nunchaku combat.
Opposite page, below: an overhead scoring strike.
Above right: an overhead block.
Right: a side block against a sideways strike.

help from a specialist in judo, a teacher of kung fu and a jujutsu expert he produced the new system, whose name means 'with the aid of this system of fist style you will achieve long life and happiness'. Among the better-known American martial artists who espoused the style were Al Dacascos and Al Reyes. Although it is a newly developed art, kaju-kenbo has a system of kata, increasingly difficult techniques and other ideas reminiscent of the older styles. One of these is called the 'clock system', in which all the directions from the centre point of a circle to the numbers on a clock are used as possible defence and counterattacking directions.

Mu tau is another form of hybrid, involving the blending of ancient Greek fighting methods with modern martial arts. The gladiatorial contests recreated in the film *Spartacus*, and the Olympic pancratium, meaning 'all powers', are reminders that in the days of ancient Rome and Greece the martial arts were not neglected. The Greek pancratium was a violent contest and it was the vision of those early days plus his experience in karate which led an American, Jim Arvanitis, to evolve his mu tau style. It is a system for tough people. Like the pancratium empty-hand fights, mu tau competitions have no rounds and virtually no rules. It is an all-embracing system. The only concessions that mu tau makes to the safety-conscious times in which we live is that students wear protective armour, and there is a restriction on attacks to the knee joint, groin and spine. Students of mu tau experience almost total fighting freedom and this is its strongest appeal.

One cannot leave the hybrid scene without returning to the Bruce Lee phenomenon. Criticized and idolized, the Little Dragon, as he was affectionately called, brought out into the open an argument that had been an undercurrent of martial arts discussion for many years. Quite simply, it was the question of whether one should stick to a traditional style of training or experiment for oneself. One strand of this argument is of immense interest to anyone who studies any discipline, and that is the matter of technique and spontaneity. In the last few years of his brief life, Lee came down heavily in favour of the latter. He maintained that a martial artist should use the simplest and most obvious technique in any given situation, although the word 'technique', with its implications of a preconceived

method, would in the last analysis have been alien to his thoughts.

Lee's biographers told how he was obsessed with martial arts. He pushed himself to extraordinary lengths and had some kind of measuring machine which he attached to his body to monitor his progress. His obsession ate away at him during the final years, and to his students it was apparent that he was trying to formulate something which often appeared as a condemnation of the classical martial arts. On the positive side he was once faced by a man who wanted to know how he would fight using a stick. The man held a stick in his hand and Lee did the same. Instead of moving into a complex manoeuvre, Lee simply hit the man on the hand and he dropped the stick. This spontaneous reaction illustrated Lee's dictum: 'Explore what is useful.'

Lee counselled his students to abandon the traditional, especially where it contained useless, flowery movements, and concentrate on the practical. What he did not see, or refused to acknowledge, is that before you can discard something you must first possess it. An untaught child may fight using whatever 'methods' come to hand. Such is the nature of human beings that on future occasions he would tend to use the same methods. Subsequently, if other boys or girls asked him to give them lessons, he would teach them his methods. A great deal of experience of martial arts would be necessary before those boys or girls could consider giving up the methods they had learned in favour of spontaneity. Lee's students try to uphold his ideas, but many in fact teach a variety of styles including Thai boxing, escrima and Wing Chun-type techniques, plus methods which Lee himself used. This amalgamation is known as jeet kune do (see page 141).

The key to Lee's ideas lies in an understanding of human physiology and the levels of energy and intelligence found within it. Spontaneity of action is a kind of instantaneous discovery coming from the 'intelligence' of the body. For example, faced with the parts of a table which you must fit together without the aid of printed instructions, you may wonder what to do. You look at the different pieces, and suddenly you 'see' how it works. Are you calling on past experience? Not entirely. There is something new at work which is neither memory nor experience. At the simplest level a child can 'see' that square pegs fit in square holes. But this capacity for seeing is not present all the time, it needs some extra stimulus. Mainly one acts from habit, instead of re-evaluating each situation. It is probably this awareness of the immediate present that Lee was striving to attain, and which those who wish to follow his thinking need to achieve, somehow.

INDIAN MARTIAL ARTS

The martial arts of India go back to far distant times. This has been demonstrated in recent years by the British theatre director Peter Brook, whose presentation of the Indian epic the *Mahabharata* featured many of these arts. The *Mahabharata* is many times longer than the Bible, and part of it deals with the war between rival members of a noble family. Philosophical and religious themes run through the entire story and show that no aspect of Indian culture can be separated from an awareness of the presence of the divine. When the hero of the battle, Arjuna, asks his wise advisor, Krishna, how anyone can take up arms against his own flesh and blood, Krishna begins to teach him 'the way of action without attachment to action'. This teaching is similar to Buddhist and Taoist teachings which point to the idea of being in the world but not of the world.

The South Indian art of kalari, which is practised in the small state of Kerala, illustrates this metaphysical dimension. Students arrive for training in the early morning, ritually oiled and wearing a 2-metre length of cotton cloth or kacha wrapped firmly round their waists. As in many Chinese martial arts, the directions of the compass are significant in the specially constructed training area which always measures 21 feet (6.4 metres) from east to west, and 42 feet (12.8 metres) from north to south. Work begins and ends at the entrance to the area, in the middle of the east wall. On entering, a student lifts his right leg and moves it in a clockwise direction across the threshold. He then touches the ground with his right hand, to evoke the earth goddess, an acknowledgement that during the session she will be stamped upon many times. This is followed by a second gesture with the right hand: the student touches his forehead to show reverence to the deities who impart knowledge. The monkey god, Hanuman, who represents physical strength, is remembered by a touch on the left knee with the right hand and on the right knee with the left hand. Finally, after counting to 30, the student raises his hands to touch his shoulders in honour of Garuda, a god of strength who lives in the air. In some kalari schools prostrations are made in different directions to do homage to still more deities.

Where the southern wall meets the western wall is the most significant place in the training area, for it is here that destruction meets peace. On this spot a six-tier sand castle or poothara is always constructed, tapering to a point. The first five tiers represent the five senses and the sixth tier represents the mind–intellect. The highest point of the castle is associated with the god Siva and the goddess Devi, the ideal couple through whom all things in life are fulfilled and maintained. Flowers, leaves, oil lamps, a mirror and a conch shell decorate the training space. The conch shell is blown at the beginning and end of each session. The most ancient symbols of kalari are a stool and a pair of sandals, which are placed in front of the sand castle to show respect for the long line of kalari teachers, the gurukkals, who preserved and transmitted the art in pure form for many centuries.

Left: holding aloft the curved sticks, or otta, in a moment of combat.
Right: displaying the flexible sword-belt or urumi.

Above: *action involving the kettukari or cane; note the deep stance.*

Below: *the straight stick or muchan is a powerful weapon. It is shown here in a cutting action which is being blocked.*

This awareness of the presence of the divine, in many forms, imbues the movements of kalari students with a quality which is not found in many other martial arts of the East. It is difficult to describe but the student seems to be communicating the idea that he is not alone; the divine is with him.

The techniques of the art are preserved on palm leaf manuscripts, which are closely guarded. The formal verbal and written instruction which we in the West take for granted is not used by the teachers; students must learn by observation. Talking, even about injuries sustained and their consequences and treatment, is not encouraged. Until he becomes a teacher himself, a student has no access to manuals; he must rely on memory.

Through experience a student learns much about his own body and what will best prepare it for training. No food is taken before the session begins, and afterwards a special soup, marunmu-kanji, is drunk.

As in all Chinese and Japanese martial arts, kalari students are taught that the centre of energy is located a little below the navel and they study how

Left and below: *intricate grappling techniques, or kattaram, involving locks and catching methods.*

*Above: the mighty club or gada
produces tremendous impact.
Opposite page: two exponents of
kalari crouch very low, holding the
otta in an unusual two-handed grip.*

to focus their strength in that area. One usually takes
the placing of the feet on the ground for granted, but
in kalari the feet are put on the ground in a special
way as one moves. Continuous actions sometimes
incorporate as many as 12 foot positions. Animal
gestures form part of the syllabus, both as a means
of attack and of defence. Striking and kicking,
wrestling and locking techniques are also included.

It has been estimated that India has the widest
range of martial arts weapons of any country in
the world and about a dozen are taught in kalari.
These include a long sword, a dagger, a straight
stick, a curved stick, a huge mace, a cane and a
spear. Local carpenters and blacksmiths maintain
close ties with kalari exponents and furnish them
with the weapons they need. Weapons training
can begin once the student is conversant with the
empty-hand methods.

Although kalari has so many religious threads
running through it, it has become totally distinct
from any religious or educational organization;
possibly this break has been made to maintain the art
intact and free from the influence of bureaucrats.

During the long years of British rule in India,
many Western methods of self-defence were introduced. At the beginning of this century, the police
and army were taught a system of crowd control and
fighting using a long walking stick or heavy cane
called a lathi. It is still used today, with devastating
effect. The system was built up using methods
brought from the West Indies and others derived
from the French cane (see savate, page 186). To
wield a lathi one needs supple shoulders and wrists,
and a knowledge of vital spots on the body.

Throughout India, wrestling has always been

popular. Its recorded history begins in the twelfth
century AD with the style called vajra-musti. Surprisingly, it was initially reserved for members of
the Brahmin caste, the highest social group in India,
although one would have thought that it would have
been found among the ranks of the Kshatriya or
warrior caste. Some researchers say that
Bodhidharma himself (see page 99) was from this
caste. Vajra-musti is the most violent form of
wrestling and in modern times matches between
exponents of this style have been infrequent,
because of the damage caused to the participants.

The courts of the Indian princes included
wrestlers and teachers of wrestling and European
accounts of contests describe them as bloody. The
modern writer Robert Smith gives the title 'father
of Indian athletics' to a seventeenth-century
wrestler called Ramdas, but with the incursion of
the British in the eighteenth century both wrestling
and athletics went into a decline. In the following
century the decline was reversed and by 1900
Indian wrestlers were to be seen in the West com-
peting for honours. The hero of Indian wrestling
at this time was Gama, from Kashmir. When he
came to Europe the world-famous wrestler Hack-
enschmidt declined to meet him, but an equally
famous American, Frank Gotch, fought him to a
draw. *The Times* stated that all European wrestlers
'were hiding in the Swiss mountains or in Berlin',
but a Pole called Zbyszco faced the Indian in
Shepherd's Bush, London. After several hours
neither man had won, and the match was post-
poned until the following day. The Pole did not
show up for the sequel, so Gama was declared the
winner. Later, a return contest was staged in India,
and this time Gama won. One press report stated
that Zbyszco 'was about as much use in the hands
of Gama as Fay Wray in the hands of King Kong'.

The training of an Indian wrestler puts the
training for sumo (see page 78) in the shade.

According to Robert Smith the daily schedule including brief rests and massage, lasts from three o'clock in the morning until eight o'clock at night. Running and weightlifting are part of the training, although most of the students' time is spent learning wrestling techniques.

One of India's strangest weapons is the Bundi dagger consisting of a straight tapering blade, a pistol-type grip and two long guards formed from metal strips, which protect the upper and lower sides of the fist and forearm. Training in the use of this weapon includes a study of the vital target areas on the human body.

In India, study of the various martial arts goes hand in hand with the study of healing. This often means that a teacher is also a healer, and the use of herbs, diet, massage, and specific massage oils for specific curative purposes, is widespread. While we in the West tend to use massage oil merely as a lubricant or to soothe muscles, the ingredients of Indian oils vary greatly, are absorbed by the body and produce visible results. Many healers have their own secret ingredients which they only reveal to a trustworthy disciple. A striking form of Indian massage involves lying the patient down on the floor and, using a rope suspended from an overhead beam, walking on him or her, while holding on to the rope to regulate the weight given to each step. This massage is used on patients suffering from a wide variety of illnesses as well as martial arts injuries.

Early in the first millennium, Buddhist missionaries travelled from China to Ceylon (Sri Lanka). The researcher R. A. Vairamuttu has written that this contact led to the importing of various Chinese martial arts into the country, the most prominent being chin-na or cheena-adi, as Vairamuttu calls it. Several researchers believe that this Chinese art was the basis for Japanese jujutsu (see page 32), as it involves seizing and damaging the vital points of the body. In Ceylon chin-na was seen as an adjunct to wrestling techniques, and was also used as a method of arresting criminals.

As almost no written evidence has come to light concerning the earliest days of this art in Ceylon, or in India where it was sporadically practised, one must rely on modern expositions of the system for information. The best-known exponent of chin-na in the West today is Dr Yang Jwingming of the United States. He teaches that chin-na techniques are divided into five groups: those which attack the muscles, those which displace the bones, those which impede the breath, those which close the arteries and those which attack the chan-

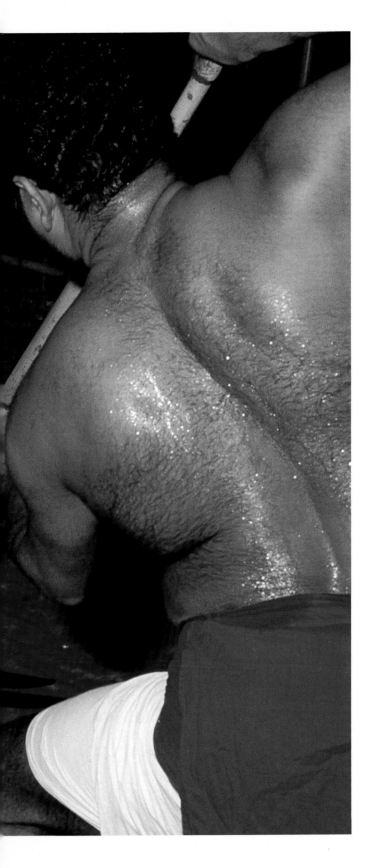

nels (chinglo) of acupuncture. The most widely known of these and the most misunderstood is the closing of the artery technique, called popularly, dim muk or the death touch. Current belief about this technique says that with its use one may strike or press certain vital spots on the body without apparently injuring the person at the time. Later, he will become paralysed or will die. Experts, so it is said, can even schedule the time of the victim's death, so that they will be far from the scene and have an alibi when it occurs. This uninformed notion comes from a mish-mash of magazine articles and books written to impress the gullible. Yang himself only skirts round the question and points out that even the rudiments of the technique can only be taught under close supervision. A pre-requiste for its correct performance, he says, is the possession of a good store of jing or vital energy on the part of the performer, which means that he must be a disciplined and mature individual. Jing, one of the many Chinese terms for vital energy, can be equated with an accumulation of what in hatha yoga is referred to as prana, although this is an oversimplification of a wide topic.

The principal element in chin-na, from the point of view of effectiveness, is surprise. While this is in a sense true of all martial arts, it is singularly true of the art of seizing, since, if the first attempt is ineffective, the victim can strike back. Once he is tensed up and fighting, his body is much less manageable, his muscles are hardened against finger grips, and the attacker must think about defending himself.

Some years ago a BBC team visited southern India and revealed that many of the movements of the Bharata Natyam style of dancing contained steps and arm movements akin to martial arts styles. This graceful art seems to be as far from fighting as one can imagine, but the relationship underlines what a survey of the martial arts of the world suggests: that combat and dance are often very close.

The Indian wrestler, working for 16 hours a day on his physique and method, struggles with himself to continue such a regime. The kalari martial artist struggles with his opponent and at the same time tries to maintain an awareness of the divine. The dancer portrays struggle and simultaneously strives to follow the exacting movements he or she has been taught. At its best therefore, a martial art is not about destroying or injuring a human being, but reflects the universal struggle or effort which maintains the whole of creation.

The man on the right holds a kuntham or spear, which his opponent has parried with his sword, the other hand gripping a shield.

ACKNOWLEDGEMENTS

The following martial artists posed for the photographs:

Karate – Graham Smith, Robert Smith
Judo – Brian Dossett, Adrian Langan
Aikido – Brian Dossett, Adrian Langan
Jujutsu – James Shortt, Willy Gatt
Kendo – Jock Hopson, Len Bean
Iaido – Jock Hopson, Len Bean
Kyudo – Melanie Spriggs, Don Slade Southam, John Carder Bush
Ryukyu kobujutsu – Julian Mead, Roger Parker
Ninjutsu – David Heald, Christopher Nice
Shorinji Kempo – Tameo Mizuno, S. K. Jee, Paul White
Jodo – Jock Hopson, Len Bean
Shaolin kung fu – Robert Stannells, Kelvyn Liew, Kok Sian
T'ai chi – Louanne Richards, Paul Crompton
Pakua and hsing-i – Raymond Wilkie, Barry Evans
Wushu – Sean Dervan, Gerard Dervan
Wing Chun and escrima – Nino Bernardo, Luc Ribouet, Segun Johnson
Pentjak silat – Glenn Lobo, Dominic Taylor
Taekwondo – Jim Eldon, Kumi Eldon
Kick boxing – Mustapha Hussein, Chris Husband
Savate – Phil Reed, Mounir Badreddine
Nunchaku combat – Brian Dossett, Adrian Langan

The views expressed in this book are those of the author and are not necessarily those of the people appearing in the photographs.

The author would like to thank all those who so kindly took part in the photographic sessions, Hrut Keshishian for information on Indian martial arts, and Lars Petersen for his help in organizing photography in Japan.

INDEX

Japanese and Chinese names are given in the order in which they are generally used in the Western martial arts world.

Page numbers in italics refer to illustrations.